THE CHRISTMAS COOKIE COOKBOOK

THE CHRISTMAS COOKIE COOKBOOK

ALL THE RULES AND DELICIOUS RECIPES TO START YOUR OWN HOLIDAY COOKIE CLUB

ANN PEARLMAN

AND MARYBETH BAYER

ATRIA PAPERBACK

NEW YORK   LONDON   TORONTO   SYDNEY

ATRIA PAPERBACK
A Division of Simon & Schuster, Inc.
1230 Avenue of the Americas
New York, NY 10020

Copyright © 2010 by Ann Pearlman, LLC

All rights reserved, including the right to reproduce this book or portions thereof in any form whatsoever. For information address Atria Books Subsidiary Rights Department, 1230 Avenue of the Americas, New York, NY 10020

First Atria Paperback edition October 2010

ATRIA PAPERBACK and colophon are trademarks of Simon & Schuster, Inc.

For information about special discounts for bulk purchases, please contact Simon & Schuster Special Sales at 1-866-506-1949 or business@simonandschuster.com.

The Simon & Schuster Speakers Bureau can bring authors to your live event. For more information or to book an event contact the Simon & Schuster Speakers Bureau at 1-866-248-3049 or visit our website at www.simonspeakers.com.

Designed by Davina Mock-Maniscalco

Manufactured in the United States of America

10   9   8   7   6   5   4   3   2   1

Library of Congress Cataloging-in-Publication Data is available upon request.

ISBN 978-1-4391-5954-5
ISBN 978-1-4391-7693-1 (ebook)

To cookie clubs . . .
may the yeast of joy and friendship expand our lives

Contents

THE CHRISTMAS COOKIE COOKBOOK

Confessions of a Cookie Virgin

I HAD NEVER HEARD OF cookie exchanges until I met Marybeth. We joined the same woman's investment club back in the late nineties and discovered we had lots of interests in common. We both loved to dance, read books, go to concerts, socialize, dine out, and cook. When she moved around the corner from me, we spent even more time together! As soon as I heard about her cookie party, I wanted to join. I listened as our friends laughed about funny events, discussed what cookies they might bake, and joked about the rules.

"I want to come," I said, but they shook their heads.

"Nope. We have rules. Only twelve people. So someone will have to drop out."

"Twelve? Why only twelve?" I pushed.

"'Cause we don't want to bake more than 13 dozen cookies!"

"Thirteen dozen? If there are only twelve women?"

"We each donate one dozen to charity, Safe House." That completely sold me. The fact that I would be making something for families going through hard times *and* partying with my girlfriends increased my desire to attend. Well, maybe some year I'd be able to come. Maybe I could even start my own group.

Finally, someone dropped out. There was room for me.

I was thrilled.

But I was nervous! I love to bake, but I heard about the standards of delicious cookies in fabulous packages and wondered if mine would taste sufficiently yummy, be sufficiently attractive. And the cookies had to come with a story! What kind of story? I immediately thought of baking my grandmother's pecan balls, the favorite cookie of my entire family and one that held memories of me and my grandmother in her kitchen. But there was no story: no hero, no conflict, no quest, no crisis. Only happy memories and always the happy ending of delicious cookies.

"That's enough," Marybeth assured. "Family recipes with memories are the best cookie stories."

Then I shopped to buy packaging that might be acceptable. I went to party supply stores, craft stores, department stores. I looked at tins and baker's boxes. Finally I chose small brown paper bags and decorated the handles with raffia and bronze wired ribbon.

I relinquished the idea of baking watermelon rind fruitcakes loaded with amaretto, which I love, but which my children do not. The weekend after Thanksgiving, I baked cookies instead of fruitcakes. And as I was rolling the warm cookies with their nutty and buttery aroma in feathery confectioners' sugar, I was brought back to my grandmother's kitchen with the laughing lady cookie canister and remembered how she taught me to sift the sugar over the mounds of cookies to let it soak in.

The party was full of great cheer, fun, fabulous food, joking, and good-natured teasing. I didn't know all the women at the first party and thus was introduced to women who eventually became new friends. When it was my turn to pass out my cookies and tell my story, I was nervous. But my new friends were welcoming and wanted to hear more about my grandmother Lala. They liked my packaging and loved the cookies. I was no longer a cookie virgin! And I was accepted into the fold of fun-loving cookie bakers. Through the party I developed a group of friends I socialize with all year.

I returned home with 12 dozen cookies, which I shared with friends and family alike. My kids and grandkids tasted them, each immediately developing a favorite. At the yearly yoga party I attend, the guests marveled at the homemade delicious cookies. I got a call from the hostess of the Chanukah party wanting recipes. Of course I saved a few dozen for Christmas Day to be nibbled on in between present opening. Now everyone always knows when the cookie party is and they all come over to taste the goodies.

The Christmas cookie night became the highlight of my winter holiday season, a party that I looked forward to throughout the year. I also knew, from the first time I attended, that it would make a terrific setting for a book about women's friendships. The seed of my novel, *The Christmas Cookie Club*, was planted. Once the draft was written, Marybeth and I started dreaming about writing a book on how to throw your own cookie party, which became the book you are now reading.

• • •

BUT I HAD NO IDEA the phenomenon that would surround me. Since *The Christmas Cookie Club* hit the stands, I have felt like I've been at the forefront of a movement I did not even know existed. Across the country I've been swarmed with people excited to tell me about their cookie exchanges. And I've been amazed by the number, the variety, and, of course, the importance of them to the participants.

In Greenville, South Carolina, I met an independent bookstore owner whose cookie party has been meeting for thirty years. Now, there are three generations in that club! In St. Joseph, Michigan, I met a group of women who had read my book for their book club and happened to be away on a girlfriends' weekend. They had no idea I'd be at a bookstore in the area. I signed books for them, and then all of us signed one for the hostess of their cookie exchange. At another reading, a woman sent her daughter to get a book signed for her. Her mom had been in an exchange, the highlight of her winter season, for decades. Unfortunately, she was now in a walker, but her daughter retrieved a book for her.

There are cookie parties where all the cookies are eaten by the end of the party. (Of course the attendees don't each bring 13 dozen cookies!) Some are co-ed, some are all men, some are extended family parties. In several, a group gets together to bake or exchange kitchen gadgets in drawings and white elephant games. And cookie clubs spring up from social groups, work groups, church groups, neighborhoods, and families.

I'VE HEARD FROM A LOT of people how a Christmas cookie club has helped them through hard times. Peggy, a teacher, e-mailed me that the holiday season was difficult because her husband had died right after Thanksgiving the year before. Joannie, a new teacher from China, joined her school's staff and mentioned that there was a muffin tin left in the apartment she rented. She had no idea what to do with it and didn't understand American baking. Peggy offered to help, and taught her how to make orange-ginger muffins and peanut butter cookies. The next time they got together, they made pumpkin banana muffins and gingerbread boys. And then right before Christmas, Joannie brought two friends recently arrived from China and Peggy taught them how to make and decorate Christmas cutout cookies for the first time. Most unusual cross-cultural cookie virgins! It was just the experience Peggy needed to put her in the holiday mood!

And then right after Christmas of last year a special connection was made that was close to home. It's about Daphne, one of my friends and one of the original cookie sisters. I had folded parts of her life—the circumstances regarding the tragedy of her son's death—in the chapter about Charlene. Unfortunately, at this year's cookie club, Daphne announced that she was moving to Texas to be closer to two of her children, both quarterhorse trainers, and to accept a huge promotion. Car loaded, she was driving when she got a call from her sister-in-law.

"Do you know a Melody Mead Parker?"

Before Daphne could answer, her sister-in-law said, "She says she's your sister and has been looking for you for years. Here's her telephone number."

Daphne immediately dialed it.

Melody and her two brothers were from Daphne's father's second marriage. She remembers Melody as her cute little shadow, following her around. Every morning she and her two brothers jumped on Daphne's bed and snuggled up with her. But her father's new wife never liked Daphne; after all, she was the off-spring of a previous marriage, the proof of a previous love. So when visitation stopped, they drifted apart.

The last time Daphne saw Melody was twenty-five years earlier, when Melody was a young teen.

Years passed and Daphne tried to find her siblings, but she finally gave up. Hers was a military family and they moved often. She went through life as if an only child, but aware she had siblings somewhere, siblings she had lost.

Meanwhile, Melody and her brothers struggled to find Daphne, but Daphne had married and divorced and remarried, changing her name and moving so that she was impossible to find. Melody did an online search in 1995 to find Daphne, but came up with 30 people with the same name. Daphne did the same, but she also hit a wall of too many names, too many places, and changed names.

So the two separated sisters attempted to find each other, and gave up. The years marched on. A quarter of a century passed.

And then Melody ran Daphne's name through the Internet one more time, and there was an article on *The Christmas Cookie Club* mentioning Daphne, her son's death, and her location.

Melody was also driving when her cell phone rang. She immediately recognized Daphne's voice. Within minutes the two pulled over to the side of their respective highways, stretched across half the United States, and started bawling. Melody described losing Daphne, and how she always knew she was out there and how she lived with an ache in her heart. And Daphne told Melody about life lived as an only child when she had three siblings in the world.

"My girlfriend wrote that book," Daphne said.

"I know, that's how I found you. I hope the story about your son wasn't true."

"It is. But because of that, I found you again."

When I talked to Daphne she said, "So your book reunited a family. Amazing how things work. It's the mystery of life that's so wonderful and oftentimes overlooked. This is a Christmas miracle that came from a lovely Christmas book."

We love our party so much that Marybeth and I wrote this workbook to help you start your own. The possibilities for parties are endless: there could be Chanukah, Ramadan, and Valentine's Day cookie parties. We want you to develop a new ritual to have with your friends, family, or community. Cookie parties are an inexpensive way to contribute and give to those we care about. And each one, no matter its form, is anticipated merriment! Bonds are built by sharing fun and stories, both of which inevitably touch our lives. We wrote this together and so there are stories from both of our families and friends. These are our tips, ideas, and recipes for throwing your own great cookie party and cultivating a new holiday tradition. Enjoy!

ONE

Starting Your Own Party

THIS BOOK WILL OUTLINE all of the how-to's for starting your own cookie party, from choosing the guests and recipes to the crowning glory when the cookies are passed out and each member ends up with 12 dozen different homemade cookies to take home and share with families, friends, and neighbors. Our cookie party developed over eighteen years into what it is now. The year 2010 will be its twentieth anniversary! The party evolved from year to year as we made changes to accommodate all of us, fine-tuning each event, casting aside things that didn't work so well, and incorporating new ideas that were terrific. Now you're getting the benefit of our years of trial and error by reading this book. You'll have advance knowledge of what will make your party successful so it can grow into a treasured tradition.

THE EVOLUTION OF THE PARTY

I'VE MADE COOKIES EVERY YEAR for most of my life. When I was a child, I started making Christmas cutouts for my family. There were seven children in my family and my mom was super busy just taking care of us. She made wedding cakes for extra money, and became so well-known for her delicious lemon cakes that they were bought for many occasions in addition to weddings, like graduation parties and anniversary parties. Honestly, Mom didn't bake us cookies, cakes, and pies, not for lack of desire, but she simply didn't have the extra time. I was the one who made pies with homemade pie crusts. We had a cherry tree in our yard, and every summer, usually around the Fourth of July, we would pick all the cherries. I would make seven or eight pies for our family. We ate one or two as soon as soon as they came out of the oven and froze the rest for when we wanted a reminder of summer.

When I asked for cookies, Mom showed me the cookbook and let me try my best. By doing it that way, she expressed confidence in my baking ability. It's no surprise that my early versions of cutouts were a little on the thick side! But my sisters and I decorated them with frosting for the holidays and, along with my brothers, gobbled them up without even noticing they weren't thin and elegant. They tasted delicious. I suspect my love of baking started with seeing my family devour my pies and cookies!

In my twenties, I continued the tradition with a girlfriend. We'd get together for an evening or two and we'd mix up and bake about eight or nine kinds of cookies. It took hours to bake and organize all those different batches. We had lots of fun, laughing and joking as we stirred and cooked. Of course, we'd pour a glass or two of wine and as the night went on the baking became more infused with laughter, jokes, and intimate conversation. Sometimes, while our children slept, we stayed up all night baking. Then, one year I was invited to a cookie exchange. I had never heard of a holiday cookie exchange. At that particular party, each guest brought one dozen cookies to share. When I arrived, there were twenty other women and each carried a plate of cookies. All the cookies were arranged on a table. Another table was filled with hors d'oeuvres and wine and we spent the evening socializing. At the end of the evening, each guest went to the table and chose a dozen different cookies to take home. I remember thinking, "This is so great!"

I loved the idea that a group of women gathered together, shared cookies and recipes, and got to know one another. But a dozen cookies with my large family didn't do the trick! I wanted to expand the concept so we each brought more cookies to the exchange and were able to return home with all the cookies we needed for the holiday season. The first exchange I hosted was more like an open house, and many of the women who came didn't know one another. It became a great way for my girlfriends to meet each other. I couldn't invite every woman I knew, but chose guests based on their love and interest in baking cookies. I also talked with each prospective guest to find out if she would enjoy the idea of sharing cookie recipes with others. My idea was to ask my cookie ladies to bake a favorite family recipe and then share the source of the recipe. I also thought we could talk about the special memories attached to that cookie.

Why did I want to do it this way?

I was recently divorced, a single mother, and needed to form new traditions to celebrate the holidays. I guess I wanted to broaden my definition of family to include my friends. So the breakup of my marriage was the stimulus for the cookie party. I invited a bunch of old friends and some of my sisters to my first party. All the guests loved it, and from that point a cookie party legend was born, and, in the process, a beloved annual tradition was cemented in my life.

YOUR WONDERFUL GUESTS!

THE MOST IMPORTANT ASPECT OF a cookie party is your guests and the fun you are going to have together. My cookie party is really about women giving to each other. It's a celebration of girlfriends, and the party itself helps seal the bond. So choose women who know each other, or who you think will enjoy each other, and who like to bake. Several of the women who are with me today have been with me since my first party. Somewhere along the way, we started joking that we were the "cookie bitches." I'm not sure how that appellation came to be. Maybe it was because I was teased for rules and became the cookie bitch. Then, I was promoted to the head cookie bitch. It seems that groups often turn a negative term into an endearing positive for use only within the group. If anyone else calls us that . . . beware. But within the group it's all about love and belonging. Now the word encompasses all my wonderful ladies at the cookie party.

When I add a member (now I have a list of people *waiting* to be part of the exchange), I make sure she will enjoy both the women who are already members, and also baking cookies. New guests bring new recipes, creativity, and enthusiasm. And our new friends gather with us in other events throughout the year. These are important elements. Unfortunately, no matter how much I enjoy someone, or how much my other cookie bitches like and have fun with her, she won't make a great addition to the party if she hates baking. Sometimes, a friend will try because she so wants to be part of the fun. But if she hates having to cook 13 dozen of the same cookie, it won't work. She'll be miserable thinking about the party preparations. It will be drudgery for her, while for the rest of us it's so much a part of the fun.

There are other ways to include friends who don't want to be part of the exchange. I have a good friend who tried it but left because she didn't like baking. She is now our party photographer. I always give her a cookie tin full of that year's treasure trove as a form of payment for her services. The most important ingredient in the party is the love and good cheer that is shared. Cookies, though we all want them to be delicious and very presentable as gifts, are the excuse that brings us all together.

I never wanted to have an exclusive party where any woman felt unwanted or left out. That smacked of those cliques in middle school and high school that could be so demoralizing. We were certainly way beyond that petty insecurity and hurt. Yet there's a limit to how many dozens of cookies we're willing to bake. I started with twelve women. There were times when I added one or two extra women, but the group felt it was too many. My own party members insisted that we keep the group at an even twelve. They didn't want to bake more than 13 dozen of the same cookie. I have bowed to this rule faithfully. However, other people hear about my party and want to be a part of it and I can't extend an invitation to them because I am limited to twelve. I add them to my waiting list, and every so often I have an opening in the party to offer to a new cookie bitch.

I have suggested that people form their own parties. Several women told me they want to be a part of my cookie exchange because they've heard about the fun we have and have tasted the great cookies we give one another. I hope this book will show them, and you, how to duplicate the party so anyone who wants a party can plan it.

So, how do you find twelve women to begin your very own cookie party? This was a process for me. I included from the start my closest girlfriends. The friends who baked cookies with me during those all night sessions were my first members. We had so much fun baking together, listening to music, eating yummy appetizers; I just expanded on that idea. I invited people I met as I lived my life the rest of the year. Two members I met in my investment club. One of my sisters was a member for a few years until she moved out of state. Some guests left the state but still make it back to the cookie party every year. One of my dearest friends even comes from Virginia every year to be a part of this group of women! It gives her a chance to see all her old girlfriends for a loving reunion.

So what is it about us that make this party so special? It's that we love each other, know each other, and share this wonderful night together. All the years together have increased our knowledge and comfort with each other, cementing our bonds. We are all very complex women who have busy, complicated lives. All of us work outside the home. Some are self-employed. Some are single; some are married; some have children. We are gregarious, friendly, love to try new things, and appreciate an additional excuse to get together for food and wine and laughs. We are grateful for our girlfriends. This group is an all-women's group. But I do not think a cookie exchange has to be all women. It could be couples, or all men. I would love to see that!!

DARING TO SET A DATE!

GENERALLY, THE FIRST THING I do is decide on a date. The first year it was chaos trying to find a date that would work for everyone because I invited people at the last minute. After spending hours on the phone checking times with a group of people with busy schedules, I realized it would be better to pick a date that would work every year. Therefore, we chose the first Monday of December so everyone knows a year in advance and doesn't make any plans for that Monday because that is THE COOKIE PARTY. The only time that particular rule changes is when the first Monday falls immediately after Thanksgiving. We have tried a couple of times to cook on the weekend after Thanksgiving and it turns out to be too hectic. So, on the years that the first Monday of December falls after Thanksgiving, we move it to the following Monday. With all of our busy lives and schedules, it's easier to pick a recurring date that everyone knows so we can plan around it. The early date has helped make the cookie party extra special because it's the first big event that we attend for the holidays. So the cookie party kicks off the holiday season!

The fact that it's early has an additional advantage. Our cookie baking is complete. We actually start searching for our recipes in the summertime. Because so many of us socialize together, I've even overheard some of my cookie bitches talk about what they are thinking about baking during an Independence Day party! Or they'll ask me what I think would be yummier, an apricot thumbprint or a lemon shortbread? Because we're all so conscientious about the quality of our cookies, we're very serious about deciding which cookie we're going to present each year. I start buying cookie magazines and watching food shows that deal with cookies to get new ideas for both the cookie and packaging too!

COOKIES, COOKIES, COOKIES!

IF A NEW COOKIE BITCH—LOVINGLY called a cookie virgin—is uncertain about a recipe, she'll generally ask me if it'll work. My friends are serious about the cookie recipes, so my style is to be reassuring rather than critical about the cookies. If they see a cookie recipe in a magazine or cookbook, they make a note of it and consider it for the cookie party. We do the hunting and gathering for the perfect treat long before I send out the invitations. Some of us have probably tried a couple of recipes, maybe we've been served a cookie that we love, and bug the hostess for the recipe. We all love being creative and take pride in our cookies.

Over the course of 20 years I have exhausted my supply of family recipes; however, occasionally I will remake a recipe that was very popular. For example, one of the recipes that I use every year is peanut brittle. I have a wonderful family recipe that I've made for years and have never given out. It was our sacred family peanut brittle recipe. However, that recipe is actually in this book so you have the opportunity to make it if you love peanut brittle. Because I have baked all my recipes, I scour various holiday magazines and books for new ideas. I tend to lead by example and never allow myself to make just a plain Jane cookie but pick something that is fairly spectacular and that takes some work and fussing. I hold myself to high standards: to make the absolute best cookie every year. So, I often make two or three different cookies in the very beginning of the season before I choose the cookie to bake for the cookie party. One year I also made truffles for the party, and that recipe is in this book. That year I made four different kinds of truffles and everyone received all four varieties of truffles in cute little boxes. This was time-consuming, intensive work, but they were beautiful and very well received. I enjoy every minute that I spend on the preparation and presentation, and put on music and dance while I'm cooking. I love to please other people and get pleasure from their enthusiastic appreciation.

Regardless of how many women you invite, each party member brings one dozen cookies for every other member. This is the basis for how and why this party works out so well. It sounds daunting to bake dozens and dozens of cookies, but I'll let you in on a little secret—it is infinitely easier to make several dozen of one recipe than it is to make several recipes that take a variety of ingredients, different preparation, and baking times. When I was baking cookies by myself, I would end up with as many cookies as I could bake in that evening. Because of the cookie party I know I am going to end up with 12 dozen cookies.

ENTICING INVITATIONS

WHEN I RUN INTO WOMEN during the summer, I'll sometimes mention the cookie I'm considering making that year. Or maybe I'll tell them about a new cookie recipe book I found. This serves as a reminder, but also helps to hype the party. I usually start sending out invitations at the end of October or the very beginning of November. I send them via e-mail. I used to send snail mail invitations, but now everyone is reachable on the computer and that saves a lot of time. I send a notice at least four weeks in advance so we have plenty of time to prepare. The first e-mail invitation goes out as a basic welcome back and a reminder that it's time to do cookies, as well as the date and time. I also mention any changes in the party for this year, and generally ask to hear back from them confirming that they are, in fact, planning to come. We need to know if someone will not attend because we need all twelve women to take home our 12 dozen cookies. And we don't want to miss one of our friends.

THE BLESSINGS OF BEING THE HOSTESS (AND THE TRIALS, TOO)

THERE IS BOTH AN ADVANTAGE and added pressure to being the hostess of this party, and they're basically the same thing. As the hostess, I decorate my house on Thanksgiving weekend so my home is completely decorated for the party and the rest of the holiday festivities. And I mean *completely* decorated. Christmas was always a special time for my family and my parents did their utmost to create a sense of magic and excitement for us. With seven kids, we didn't have scads of presents, but what we did have is a family full of love and togetherness. It wasn't religious, although we did attend services, but the time was focused on family. We decorated the house together, even if it was construction paper chains, and popcorn and cranberry garlands. By the time we were finished, our house looked magical. The holidays were coming! The most exciting time of the year.

I've replicated that in my own home. I have a tree that I decorate using ornaments I have collected over the years. Some I've made, some were given to me as gifts from women coming to the party. I also have a couple of ornaments that were given to me by the charities we donate the cookies to each year. Those ornaments have a special meaning for me and they're added faithfully to my tree every year. Twinkle lights dance on the outside of my home along with wreaths on both my front and side doors. Quiltmaking is a hobby of mine, and I have several holiday quilts displayed here and there throughout the house. My beloved teddy bear collection is arranged with care under my tree and my growing collection of wooden Santas is placed throughout the house.

My house is small so I'm almost out of room! I've come to the sad and practical conclusion that I can't make or receive any more decorations. I can only replace and update! My house is decorated to the hilt when my guests come through the door so they know that the holidays have indeed arrived! I want them to recapture that childhood sense of magic.

As the hostess, once the work of decorating and baking is finished I can focus on the real fun: being with my friends, having small dinner parties, cocktail parties, and family gatherings. I don't have to worry about getting my baking done or the house decorated. I simply enjoy the season. It's perfect!

I have suggested moving the party around to other homes, but this idea never caught on and we've never done it. Everyone expects to come to my house, and I love having them here. So my home has become part of our tradition. I have moved two or three times over the years and they simply follow me around!!

For you newbies who will be starting your own cookie parties,

I will make a couple of suggestions. At your first gathering ask for suggestions from your guests on how the party should be structured. If you decide to move the party from house to house, decide that first year where the party will be held the following year while you are all together. Trying to figure it out by e-mail or phone the following year is too difficult and time-consuming. You could put everyone's name in a hat and draw for the next location or perhaps someone will volunteer each year.

About four to five weeks before the event, send out a reminder e-mail to confirm that all your guests will be returning. If not, you will have ample time to invite a new guest or two. Also, the guest at whose house the party will be will have plenty of time to ready her home for the upcoming festivities. I want to wish you all good luck with your new cookie party, which is sure to become a celebrated yearly event as mine has.

THE RULES!!!

ONE IMPORTANT THING ABOUT THIS party is the rules (and I get ribbed incessantly about them). Yes, we have rules, but really they're a fun way to help the party run smoothly.

* *Cookie variety.* This was the first rule we made and it was implemented to solve a specific problem. The first year of the party there weren't any rules. I just invited twelve women, I told them what we were going to do, and to bring 12 dozen cookies. It turned out that five women brought chocolate chip cookies! That night, I said, "Next year there will be

no chocolate chip and no oatmeal raisin." These are both wonderful cookies and we all love them, but they're not really holiday cookies. We make those cookies year round. Instead, guests can think about their favorite family cookie recipes. Perhaps cookies that are reminders of our childhoods and that helped to make the holidays special. Think about someone in your family who has made a wonderful cookie and make that one, because what we love is your personal family holiday recipes and stories. When something means a lot to you, it's meaningful for all of us. You get to share yourself, and, through all the telling and getting to know each other, deep and long-lasting friendships are formed.

✳ *No goo.* I have had a couple of experiences over the years when people have brought frosted cookies that were just too gooey. They don't store well, they stick to other cookies, and end up making a mess. I had to put the kibosh on these types of cookies and created a new rule. We all agree that we want cookies that can be stored for a few weeks either in our freezers or our refrigerators and gooey frosting doesn't work. You can bring bar cookies—for example, my Seven-Layer Bars. It is delicious and stores very well. Brownies don't have a very good shelf life, and they start to go stale after the first week. Because we are giving them out over the holiday season, we want cookies that are going to last for several weeks. Typically, I put my cookies in the freezer and they last the entire season.

I take them out a few hours before they're going to be eaten to let them thaw (or thaw them in the refrigerator overnight).

* *The exclusive membership.* This is a function of the fact that the majority of cookie ladies do not want to make more than 13 dozen cookies. I invite my girlfriends, and I choose women who will embrace the spirit of this cookie exchange. All of the women who are a part of my exchange love the idea that we are creating a special holiday event that we've come to cherish through the years. Other people want to join. Invite women who share the same level of commitment. Occasionally we have a cookie virgin at the party. Initially, new cookie bitches can be a little intimidated by the rules and worry that their cookies won't be "good enough." I can assure you that cookie virgins are embraced with complete acceptance and we always make a big fuss over their cookies and packaging! Without exception, all of the cookie virgins over the years have enjoyed themselves immensely and I haven't lost one yet, so not to worry! I think, in a way, that we look back on our first year with fondness and think how far we have come. Cookie virgins bring new life to the party, wonderful fresh ideas, and new cherished family recipes.

* *Commitment.* Once you are officially part of the cookie exchange, you are expected to attend every year. There have been a few times when someone

joined the group and then, after a year or two, discovered they didn't enjoy all the baking and decided to leave our party. I have always told them that they can come by to visit future cookie parties. The twelve participants realize the importance of being able to depend on each other to be there. There have been times when someone could not be at the party because of a work-related trip or personal situation. We figured out a way for them to participate from afar. They baked their cookies early and brought them prior to the party. One year one of the women even sent her cookies by Federal Express . . . it was crazy! Then I explained why this person couldn't come to our party and passed out her cookies and told her story. Usually, if it's possible, they call during the party so we can all talk. For example, one year one of the women couldn't make it and she sent her cookies as well as a poem for me to read. The poem was so sweet it brought tears to our eyes and it felt as if she were with us. She was certainly there in spirit!

* *Life membership.* One year one of the women became concerned that I wasn't going to ask her back. She had been invited every year for five years in a row, but I guess she was afraid she'd be booted out for a new friend. I reassured her and made a new rule that since she has made it to this party for five years, she would now be a Life Member. This was comforting to her, and she jokes now about how we're all stuck with her for good. All of this was done in a silly and

light-hearted way, and we have chuckled about it many times since. We don't have a sense of rejection or exclusivity as much as practicality. For the most part, what this rule really means is that the guest has melded into the group, especially if she didn't originally know many of the other women. Each cookie bitch is assured she'll be invited until she decides to leave.

* *Packaging.* The first couple of years my guests brought cookies on a paper plate, sometimes *very flimsy* paper plates, covered with plastic wrap. This simply didn't work. The cookies slid around and fell off! They could not be stored on a paper plate because they became hard and stale! And they could not be stacked; it was hard to carry 12 dozen paper plates! So the second year we started thinking about packaging, and it has added an element of fun and creativity to the exchange. Let's face it, it's a great excuse to shop! We hunt for what women love — pretty containers for our treats and goodies. We buy small tins, sweet little boxes, colorful bags, holiday towels, large cups, oven mitts, makeup cases, and small velvet purses found at the dollar store . . . anything that will get the job done and is fun and frivolous. The cookies are neatly tucked inside, sometimes in small plastic bags or wrapped with tissue paper. This helps to make each person's cookie a bit more unique. We use these containers to share the cookies with friends who are not part of the exchange, colleagues

at work, a hairstylist, or manicurist. Someone we want to thank during the holiday season receives a dozen or so cookies that are creatively packaged. It's an added benefit to get these different presents and pay it forward by passing them throughout the community. We've really come to pride ourselves on the unique presentation. I know it sounds crazy, but everyone loves the challenge. We admire the different and creative wrapping and praise each other on what we've accomplished. Not only are we getting 12 dozen delicious cookies, but they are presented as unique gifts. It is always exciting to see what everyone comes up with.

* *Share a dish.* I will go into this further in Chapter 8, but we have a potluck each year so that I don't have to cook food for everyone by myself on top of decorating the house and baking cookies. Everyone brings a bottle of wine, and a dish and/or hors d'oeuvres. You might be surprised to learn that even though there are 12 bottles of wine, much of it disappears. Since it's at my home, I generally make one or two delicious soups, a few baguettes to serve with it, along with a simple Caesar salad so that there's something hearty to eat. Then the rest of the meal is the combination of all the wonderful hors d'oeuvres and side dishes that we bring to share. Some of these recipes are also included in the book.

* *Charity.* The last really big rule is that I request all the cookie bitches to bring 13 dozen of whatever

cookie recipe they choose. That's one extra dozen cookies. We want to give each guest a dozen and of course we keep one for ourselves! The final dozen cookies go into a bag that we then donate to a charity. The last few years we have chosen our local hospice organization. They remember us from year to year and love getting our cookies, which are made available to the families of the patients. Some years ago, one of our members was spending a lot of time at hospice while her mother was dying. Toward the end, she was there around the clock. One evening, in the wee hours, she wanted something sweet to munch on. Nothing was available. She suggested that we donate our cookies to our local hospice and we've been doing it ever since. When we donate, we ask that the cookies be given to those waiting, no matter what the hour. My friend was so happy when we chose hospice because of her experience and hoped that others enduring sadness during the holiday might be able to enjoy the cookies that we provided, homemade and made with love. You can choose whatever charity is special to you. However, I did find that nursing homes are not necessarily a good choice because usually so many of the residents' families bring cookies. We have tried other charities such as Safe House Center/Domestic Violence Project and our local homeless shelter among other great charitable organizations that can really use the donation. So, this is the reason we make the extra dozen; just to be able to pass around a little bit of love. It is one of the ways that we embrace the holidays, which can be particularly stressful for those in difficult situations. And the donation makes us feel good to be sharing, which is really what the holidays are about after all—being with friends and family, and enjoying the food, the wine, and the music! I would urge you to choose a place where your cookies will be accepted with the joy with which they are baked and shared.

* *More fun.* Through the years, I've thought of different things that I wish we had done from the very beginning. For example, I wish we had started a journal that would be full of comments and reflections of past years. That would be so much fun to read over from year to year. I actually started it this past year and am looking forward to reading it in the many years to come. The same with pictures. I would have started a scrapbook much sooner and filled it with comments and photos. I had no idea that the party would become such an event that we would long for it to be memorialized. We took pictures, but they were saved in a haphazard way. When scrapbooking became popular, we started creating a couple of pages every year from the pictures, notes about funny things that people have said at the party, and recipes that we collected from that year's party.

THE PARTY!

THE PARTY STARTS AROUND 6:30 PM. Everyone brings her cookies. I have a special place to store the cookies during the party. For the first 90 minutes or so, we socialize, catching up on what everyone has been doing over the past year, eat, and drink wine. I haven't seen some of the guests since the previous year's cookie party so it always feels like a reunion when we're back together.

There's a point in the party, typically around 8:30 PM, when we start to pass out the cookies. The first year, I wasn't sure of the best method for handing them out. Remember, at the first party that I had attended, all the cookies were on the table and people just took them as they pleased. Then, at my first party, we exchanged simultaneously. It was absolutely hilarious and totally confusing as we all shouted to find out who needed which cookies. After an hour or two of chaos, everything got sorted out, but I decided then that something needed to change; this was not a good way to share the cookies. Our current method for distribution is to have each guest go one at a time. This has turned out to be an extra-special and fun part of the party, and one that enhances the closeness between the women. We each tell a story about our cookies. Somebody decides they want to go first and retrieves her cookies. That first guest returns with her beautiful packages and tell us about her cookies. Sometimes these are very funny stories; sometimes there's a sad memory attached to it, like the favorite cookie of a father-in-law who passed that year. For the most part the story is about the hunt for the perfect cookie and perhaps a funny disaster (and there frequently is one!). The story is emblematic of the year for each woman . . . or at least the week before the party!

Each guest is in the spotlight as she tells us a story about her cookie and her packaging. We *ooh* and *aah* over the cookies and packages. Sometimes, in fact most of the time, we test the cookies right then and there! We can't wait to try them once they've been described in great detail with all the ingredients and the techniques. The guest then passes her cookies to each of us and the last dozen goes into the special charity bag. Then we all applaud loudly and gleefully in support of her efforts, and of her.

This takes a couple of hours. We take our time telling the stories, passing out our cookies, taking breaks for wine, getting seconds on the food, and taking potty breaks. Naturally, we end up in side conversations or discussions throughout the evening. During this time, one of us takes notes, so at the end of the night, there are pages of funny sayings and anecdotes about the cookies. Sometimes, we reread them. It all works so beautifully!

Every so often we've been known to dance. Once all the cookies have been passed out, the music starts. Up to this point, I softly play holiday music in the background. Once the cookies have been distributed though, we want to party a bit, so I change the music to songs that are great to dance to. A tradition at this party has been that the very first song I play is Al Green's "Love and Happiness." We dance together and by ourselves.

Once we've totally exhausted ourselves, everyone starts to head home with her cookies. Believe me when I say that the husbands, boyfriends, children, and partners are waiting at the door to see what that year's cookies look and taste like.

Some of the women who now attend were there in the beginning, and we all cherish this tradition. I know that our cookie party will continue for at least another eighteen years, or until we just can't lift up our spatulas. It's not that I'm so special or that my girlfriends are, or that this is unique. We've made it work for so long by our excitement for the party, great cheer, and love of seeing one another. We share an eagerness about the gifts (the cookies!) our friends have brought. We've fine-tuned the rules so they work for us. Our cookie party has become the essence of joyfulness, support, acceptance, and girlfriendship. You will define the essence of your party in your own way. Perhaps it will celebrate the love of working together, or a special interest, or a group of couples, or a family. We hope it's a tradition you will enjoy right into your senior years and that it gives you as many wonderful memories as it has given us.

TWO

The History of the Cookie

COOKIES HAVE AN ANCIENT history stretching back to the days of the pharaohs in Egypt. They were actually created by accident. Cooks used a small amount of cake batter to test oven temperature before baking a large cake. In those days, the wood ovens or open hearth ovens did not come with a dial to set the correct temperature like today's beautiful stoves. So, to ensure that the temperature was just right, bakers tested a small amount. At that time, honey was used as a sweetener. It wasn't until later, in the Middle East, that we starting using sugar, which was cultivated in seventh-century Persia (now called Iran).

One of the earliest known cookies that remain popular today is the macaroon. There are references to the French *macaron* as early as 1611, and it is adopted from the Italian word *maccaronne*. Most likely, the French embraced the Italian recipe and from there it spread to Holland, across the channel to England, and, eventually, over the ocean to America. Thank Heavens! Early English and Dutch settlers introduced the cookie to America in the 1600s and references were found in seventeenth-century manuscripts including *Martha Washington's Booke of Cookery*. The Dutch colony was in Manhattan (originally called New Amsterdam) and it was a custom on New Year's Day to hand out *nieuwjaar koeken*, a practice that was adopted by many groups of that time. By the early 1700s, the word *koekje* was anglicized into "cookie." Following the American Revolution, people from other parts of the country came to New York City, the nation's first capital, which resulted in a widespread use of the term. Thus the word became part of the American language.

With the development of the spice trade, cooking techniques and ingredients spread into Europe. By the fourteenth century they were common throughout Europe, from high society to street vendors. An early, popular cookie that traveled well is the jumble: a mixture of nuts, sweetener, and water. It was popular on every continent and had a similar name in each language. In 1796, the very first published American cookbook (with a long title as was common at that time, *American Cookery: or the Art of Dressing Viands, Fish, Poultry and Vegetables, and the Best Modes of Making Puff-Pastes, Pies, Tarts, Puddings, Custards and Preserves; and All Kinds of Cakes, from the Imperial Plumb to Plain Cake*) by Amelia Simmons, listed just two cookie recipes.

During the seventeenth, eighteenth, and nineteenth centuries, most cookies were made in home kitchens and usually only as a special treat due to the cost of sweeteners. Gingerbread was relatively inexpensive, easy to make, and became all the rage. The two basic forms of gingerbread are shortbread made with molasses, which originated in Scotland, and *lebkuchen*, which uses honey as a sweetener and originated in Germany. These evolved to gingersnaps with their crispy texture and crinkly tops. The first recipe for oatmeal cookies was printed in a cookbook called *The Boston Cooking-School Cook Book*, published in 1896. The Quaker Oats Company jumped on the bandwagon by putting the recipe on their box. It became super popular, and they still have the recipe on their canister!

With the ability to regulate oven temperature in the early 1900s, America's collection of recipes grew and a wonderful new cookie was born—the peanut butter cookie. It was introduced in St. Louis in 1904 at the world's fair. Early recipes only used a small amount of peanut butter and the batter was rolled and cut into slices. It wasn't until 1937 that the recipe for today's popular cookie was published in Ruth Wakefield's *Toll House Tried and True Recipes*. That recipe called for forming peanut butter–flavored dough into balls, rolling them in sugar, and pressing them with a fork to make the crisscross pattern that is so accepted today.

Chocolate was discovered in Mexico by Spanish explorers, and was consumed as a popular drink in Europe in the seventeenth and eighteenth centuries. It came to the United States in 1765, where it continued to be consumed only as a beverage until candy bars were created in the mid-nineteenth century. Baking chocolate came into play in 1893, when Milton Hershey first produced it in Pennsylvania using a new manufacturing technique.

The most famous cookies of all, Tollhouse cookies, were invented in the 1930s. In Massachusetts, there was an inn called The Tollhouse Inn. The innkeeper was making cookies one day and—*oops*—ran out of nuts. Being resourceful, she grabbed a bar of baking chocolate and broke it into pieces. She added the chunks of chocolate to the dough and, voilà, the classic American Chocolate Chip Cookie.

Cookies have remained popular over the centuries and every country has its own word for them. In England they are called biscuits, in Spain they are *galletas*, in Italy *amaretti* or *biscotti*, and here in the United States they are the delicious, delectable, and revered cookie. The chocolate chip cookie continues its reign today as America's favorite homemade cookie.

I thought it would be fun to have a couple of recipes from earlier eras, so you will also find recipes for jumbles and macaroons in the recipe chapter. Today's basic jumble recipe is made with shortening and nuts, but you can add other ingredients like chocolate chips (or any other flavored chips), raisins (or other dried fruit), and coconut.

Now there are thousands of cookie recipes and we are limited only by our creativity. We have available for our gastronomic pleasure an enormous variety of foods and spices from around the world, and wonderful new inventions to make cooking easier. There are many options today for ingredients including cinnamon, nutmeg, cloves, chocolate chips, butterscotch chips, any kind of nut, coconut, and so on. The jumble from the 1600s has been updated since cookies today can use so many different components. It is very similar to a hermit cookie although the hermits have spices (such as cloves, nutmeg, and cinnamon).

With the expansion of transportation and refrigeration, everything has changed. We have access to more exotic ingredients like coconut. With the invention of the icebox in the 1930s, refrigerated cookies (icebox cookies) were all the rage and it is true even today. Americans alone consume over two billion cookies each year, which is about 300 cookies per person. I know that I am personally certainly worthy of being what we now call a Cookie Monster.

THREE

Types, Trips, and Tools

COOKIE TYPES

*T*HERE ARE SIX BASIC cookie styles classified by method of preparation: drop, molded (hand-formed), refrigerator, rolled, pressed, and bar.

Drop. A drop cookie is made simply by scooping up spoonfuls of dough and dropping them onto a cookie sheet. For example: chocolate chip or oatmeal raisin.

Molded (hand-formed). These cookies are usually made by taking bits of dough with your hands (squeaky clean of course!) and then shaping into balls, logs, crescents, etc. For example: Mexican wedding cakes, peanut butter cookies, or peanut butter balls.

Refrigerator. With refrigerator cookies (some say ice-box) you make the dough, form it into logs, and refrigerate until firm. Sometimes you freeze them. Then you slice and bake—so easy! Sometimes I make the logs and put them into the freezer for later use. It is a great way to whip up a quick dessert at the last minute.

Rolled. Get your rolling pin out for these cookies! You roll the dough out evenly flat and use cookie cutters to make all kinds of decorative shapes. You can decorate them *before* they're baked, with raisins, nuts, sparkly sugars, or *afterward* with icing (plain or colored) and colored sugars, chocolate, and so on. These are the traditional holiday cookies. There are many recipes for cookie cut-outs. The most common is a sugar cookie recipe. There are oodles of sugar cookie–type recipes, and I have included a couple in the recipe chapter. You may have a favorite family recipe that has been passed down. Whatever recipe you choose, you will want to chill the dough for an hour or so before rolling it out on a floured surface. This will make it much easier to use your prized collection of cookie cutters. The most important part is to have fun and be creative.

Pressed. These are fun to make by using a cookie press to push out the dough into cute shapes such as stars, flowers, and, of course, Christmas trees at holiday time. Most presses come with an array of discs to make shapes appropriate for different seasons and desires. You can also use a pastry bag with the different shaped tips at the bottom to create additional variation.

Bar. Hello brownies, lemon squares, and seven-layer bars! In bar cookies you spread the dough, or layer it into a pan, bake, and then cut into serving size pieces. These are the easiest to make. Spread 'em in a pan, bake 'em, cut 'em into squares, and eat 'em! I made the rule originally to say no bar cookies because we had some really gooey ones that were impossible to store. Now something like the Seven-Layer Bars is very storable and stackable. Therefore, we are more flexible about the no bar cookie rule.

TRICKS OF THE TRADE

I LOVE TO MAKE COOKIES and, of course, I love to eat them too. With years of practice, I have learned how to be super successful at baking cookies. Here are my baking tricks and some basic rules for baking cookies:

* Always preheat your oven at least 20 minutes before baking.

* Use cooled cookie sheets. Hot sheets can change the way your cookies bake. When you put your unbaked

cookies on a hot cookie sheet they could become thinner and not cook properly. I generally have several cookie sheets available so that I can let one cookie sheet cool and use a fresh sheet for the new batch.

✳ Gather up your ingredients for the recipe ahead of time. The whole process will go smoothly if you have your ingredients at your fingertips. By laying everything out, you will not risk putting the recipe together and miss an important ingredient. I usually set up my mixer and set out the measuring cups and spoons that I will need. Have everything ready.

✳ Bake one sheet at a time. You can put two sheets in the oven, but you need to rotate them about halfway through the baking time so they both bake evenly. I think it is just easier to bake one sheet at a time. While one sheet is baking, you can get the next sheet ready. If you use several cookie sheets, you always have one available that is cooled and ready to go.

THE TOOLS

I LOVE TO BUY KITCHEN gadgets, and over the years I have gathered a great collection. I believe that you want to have the highest quality affordable utensils. Usually, though not always, you get what you pay for and quality lasts longer and provides better overall service and satisfaction. You want to buy a utensil one time and then pass it on to your children.

$\mathcal{M}$ixer. First and foremost you need a mixer. There are two basic kinds: a hand mixer and a stand mixer. I own one of each and use them at different times. When I get ready to bake cookies, I use my stand mixer. I personally own a KitchenAid and I love it! I have used it for at least ten years, and it has always done the job. When my son was young and we wanted to bake cookies, he would ask me to get out the "cookie machine." I would pull out my trusty KitchenAid, and we would spend many hours mixing cookie dough and making chocolate chip, oatmeal, or peanut butter cookies.

When I first started baking, I used a hand mixer. It's a bit touchy adding in the dry ingredients. If you add them all at once and start mixing you could end up with flour everywhere but in the bowl, where it belongs! Instead, you should shut it off, and rest it on its back while you add the flour. Or have everything absolutely ready and measured and add it with one hand while holding the mixer with the other. Women routinely do two separate things with each hand. It's not so hard!! My first stand mixer was a Sunbeam and it had standard beaters. Over the years I changed to the KitchenAid mostly because it comes with a flat paddle beater that is easier to use with cookie dough, which can frequently be quite stiff. Mixers range in price from $10 to $400, with the hand mixers on the low end. As of June 2009, Consumer Reports still recommends the KitchenAid Classic as a best buy. It comes in about seven models and 20 colors to match any décor. They are widely available and are frequently on sale.

$\mathcal{M}$easuring spoons. Measuring spoons come in all types and sizes. You can find inexpensive plastic ones, and if you want to spend a tad more, try the stainless steel. I like the stainless steel the best. Standard sets are ⅛ teaspoon, ¼ teaspoon, ½ teaspoon, 1 teaspoon, and 1 tablespoon. Again, you can get fancier sets. I own three or four sets of measuring spoons, and when I am baking it is not uncommon for me to use them all. I have one set of spoons that have larger measurements (2 tablespoons, 1½ tablespoons, and 2 teaspoons) and use them all the time.

Rubber spatulas. It is also important to have several rubber spatulas handy. They're useful for scraping down the sides of the bowl in which you are mixing the cookie dough. You will also use them to mix ingredients such as chocolate chips or chopped nuts into your batter. Rubber spatulas come in a plethora of sizes and colors. You should have a few sizes. When purchasing them, do not get ones with plastic handles. I had one that broke and got stuck in my cookie dough.

Wooden spoons. The next handy utensils to have are wooden spoons. They come in a variety of woods. Olive wood is a favorite with a lot of cooks. I've tried maple, teak, cherry, and bamboo—all with great success. This goes against my rule that you get what you pay for. The bamboo spoon, which was also the cheapest, is my favorite! Here's what you need to know:

* Do not put wooden spoons in the dishwasher (except for the bamboo spoons—they can actually go into the dishwasher and survive).

* Do not leave your spoons soaking in water. They will swell and eventually split.

✳ *Do* treat them with oil. It is usually recommended that you use mineral oil, which can easily be found at the hardware store.

✳ New spoons will sometimes get rough after the first couple of uses. I use 300-grit sandpaper and steel wool to smooth the surface before treating with mineral oil. This is usually only necessary the first time or two.

Cookie sheets. Over the years I have tried a variety of cookie sheets and some were definitely better than others. Most cookie sheets are designed to easily hold a dozen cookies. The perfect cookie sheet is made from heavy aluminum and has a shiny, bright finish. I have tried the cookie sheets with dark finishes and they have a tendency to overcook the cookies. Look for sheets with either very low edges or no edges to ensure that heat flows evenly over the cookie. If all you have is a jelly roll pan with the one-inch sides, flip it over and cook on the bottom! Make sure your sheets are not too thin or you might end up with burnt cookies. If you spend the money for two or three excellent quality cookie sheets, they will last for many years.

A properly sized cookie sheet fits into your oven and allows at least two inches on all sides for air circulation. Generally 15 x 11-inch is a good standard size. As mentioned earlier, you want to alternate cookie sheets, using a cooled sheet each time. If that is not possible, prepare the next batch on aluminum foil and after you remove the cookie sheet from the oven and transfer the cookies to a wire rack, just slide the aluminum foil with cookies onto the cookie sheet and place it right back in the oven.

Parchment paper. Parchment paper is helpful for many things in the kitchen. I use it to line my cookie sheets. You can reuse the same piece of parchment to cook an entire batch of cookies. The cookies just slide right off the parchment paper without any problem. To make the paper stay put, spray a very thin coat of cooking spray on the cookie sheet first.

The oven. Check your oven to make sure that your temperature settings are correct by using an oven thermometer. Set your oven to 350 degrees and let it completely preheat. Check the temperature and if it is accurate, great! If it is off by 10 to 15 degrees, make adjustments. To ensure even baking, place the cookies on a rack in the center of the oven. *Always* preheat the oven so your cookies do not spread out and burn around the edges.

Wire racks. When you pull your cookies out of the oven, let them cool for a minute or two and then transfer them to a wire cooling rack. The best wire racks will have the wire close together to offer the most support.

Cookie cutters. As a child I loved to make Christmas cutouts. What child doesn't? If you do not have any cookie cutters, go buy a half dozen to start. Then add to your collection over the years. I still have a shoebox full of the very cookies cutters I had as a child. I used them with my son, and I hope he uses them with his children. There are many fun shapes to choose from. If you go into any kitchen supply store, you will find a large variety of cookie cutters such as hearts, circles, diamonds, animals, pumpkins (Halloween), bunnies (Easter), Christmas trees, every size of star you can think of, and so on. I have a set of nesting stars that you can use to make a Christmas cookie tree by using the largest star for the bottom and going in graduated order from large to small. It makes a beautiful arrangement and one that you can make from year to year.

There is really no end to what you can do with cookie cutters. I also used mine to cut out bread to make fun sandwiches for my son. Decorated cutouts are a little bit of work but they are worth it.

Cookie press. Fewer people use these than the other tools that I have discussed. Some of you might not even know what they are. Generally, they're round cylinders that come with several discs to make the various shapes. You put the dough in the back of the round cylinder and the disc in the tip. Like a caulk gun, a plunger squeezes the dough out through the disc. My preferred disc has always been the Christmas tree. The discs are easily changed so you're able to make different shapes from just one recipe. You make the dough (like for the Cream Cheese Spritz Cookies on page 117) and fill the cylinder with the soft mixture. For extra pizzazz, add flavorings like lemon, almond, or peppermint . . . the sky's the limit! You pop in a disc and voilà—cookies with just a turn of the handle. It takes just a bit of practice to get the right amount of twist so the shaped dough plops onto the cookie sheet. Hold the cookie press firmly against the cookie sheet so the dough adheres to it. The first few might look less than perfect, but I just take that dough and add it to the next batch in the press. Once you get your technique down, it goes quickly. I use colored sugars (green and red) to sprinkle on top before baking and they are the perfect bite size cookie.

• • •

Let's face it. We all love kitchen gadgets. I regularly subscribe to several cooking magazines and when they recommend a product, it's all I can do to stop myself from running out and purchasing it. But you can bake all the cookies your heart desires with a very basic set of tools. And I have! So don't think you have to go on a shopping spree to stock your kitchen with all the latest and greatest gadgets. They're like toys to those of us who love to cook and bake and it's gratifying how they simplify and beautify our baking. Treat yourself to something for your kitchen now and then and I think you'll find it does enhance the process. It's really no different than a carpenter having twelve different screwdrivers. It's not a question of need, but sometimes it makes the task a little bit easier. Soon, you will have a top-notch kitchen equipped to take on the most challenging recipes!

FOUR

Cookies, Cookies, Cookies!!!!

GREETINGS

Mix your batter gaily,
Choose a colored bowl;
Make a cheerful clatter,
Whistle as you roll!
The cookies will be better
The afternoon less long,
If you do your baking
To a tuneful song![1]

THE RECIPES INCLUDED IN this book are from our cookie party, our families, our friends, and our recipe card boxes. Here are some of our favorites:

---

[1] Beilenson, Edna, *Holiday Cookies* (New York: Peter Pauper Press, 1954).

DROP COOKIES

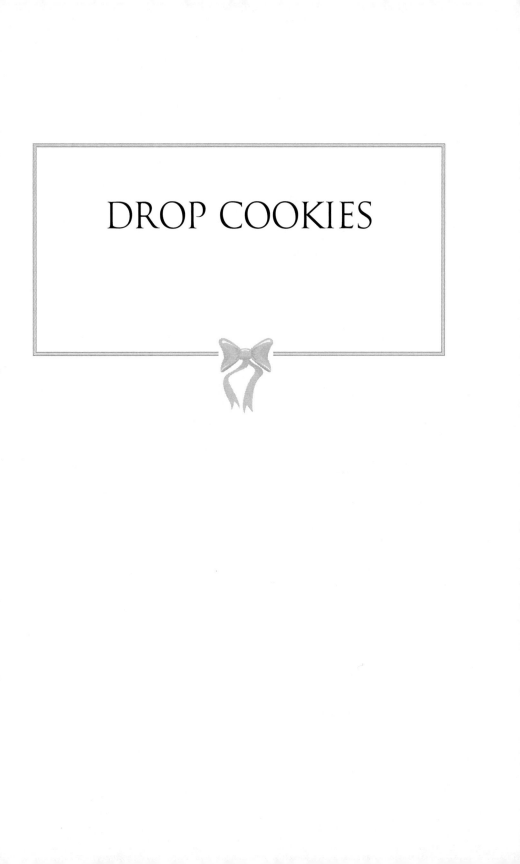

Cowboy Cookies

2 cups all-purpose flour

1 teaspoon baking soda

1 teaspoon salt

½ teaspoon baking powder

16 tablespoons (2 sticks) unsalted butter, softened

¾ cup firmly packed light brown sugar

¼ cup granulated sugar

2 large eggs

1 teaspoon pure vanilla extract

1½ cups old-fashioned oats

6 ounces semisweet chocolate, cut into ¼-inch chunks (1 cup)

¾ cup (3 ounces) pecan halves

½ cup shredded unsweetened coconut

Preheat oven to 350 degrees. Coat cookie sheets with cooking spray, line with parchment, and spray parchment.

Sift flour, baking soda, salt, and baking powder into a medium bowl.

In a large bowl, beat butter and sugars with a mixer on

medium-high until pale and creamy, about 3 minutes. Reduce speed to medium, add eggs one at a time, beating well after each addition, and beat in vanilla.

Reduce speed to low and slowly add flour mixture, beating until just incorporated. Beat in oats, chocolate, pecans, and coconut until combined (dough can be refrigerated for up to 3 days).

Using a 1½-inch ice cream scoop or a small spoon, drop dough onto cookie sheets, spacing 3 inches apart.

Bake for 11 to 13 minutes, until edges of cookies begin to brown. Transfer cookie sheets to wire rack and let cool for 5 minutes. Transfer cookies to racks to cool. Cookies can be stored up to 3 days.

Makes about 3 dozen cookies.

Cinnamon-Nut Spice Cookies

8 tablespoons (1 stick) unsalted butter, softened

1 cup plus 2 tablespoons sugar

2 teaspoons ground cinnamon

1½ teaspoons baking powder

¼ teaspoon salt

¼ teaspoon ground allspice

1 large egg

1¼ cups all-purpose flour

¾ cup coarsely chopped walnuts, toasted

Preheat oven to 350 degrees. In a large bowl, beat butter with a mixer on high for 30 seconds. Add 1 cup of the sugar, 1 teaspoon of the cinnamon, the baking powder, salt, and allspice. Beat until fluffy. Add egg and beat until combined. Gradually add flour, beating until well mixed. Stir in walnuts.

Drop dough by rounded teaspoon 2 inches apart onto an ungreased cookie sheet. In a small bowl, stir together the remaining 2 tablespoons sugar and 1 teaspoon cinnamon. Sprinkle dough mounds with sugar mixture. Bake for 11 to 13 minutes, or until edges are firm. Transfer cookies to racks, to cool.

To store, layer cookies between wax paper in an airtight storage container. Cover and store at room temperature for up to 3 days or freeze for up to 3 months.

Makes about 4 dozen cookies.

Jubilee Jumbles

8 tablespoons (1 stick) unsalted butter

1 cup firmly packed light brown sugar

½ cup granulated sugar

2 large eggs

1 cup evaporated milk

1 teaspoon pure vanilla extract

2¾ cups all-purpose flour

½ teaspoon baking soda

1 teaspoon salt

1 cup chopped pecans or walnuts

Preheat oven to 350 degrees.

In a large bowl, cream together butter and sugars. Beat in eggs. Stir in milk and vanilla.

In a medium bowl, combine flour, baking soda, salt, and nuts. Stir into batter. Chill for 1 hour.

Drop dough by rounded teaspoon 2 inches apart on a greased

cookie sheet. Bake for 10 to 12 minutes, or until bottoms are nicely browned and centers slightly firm.

Transfer cookies to racks to let cool.

(Substitute 1 cup raisins, coconut, or chocolate chips for nuts.)

Makes about 4 dozen cookies.

George's Love Cookies

(DOUBLE CHOCOLATE CHIPS)

12 tablespoons (1½ sticks) unsalted butter

¾ cup firmly packed light brown sugar

2 tablespoons milk

2 tablespoons pure vanilla extract

¼ cup unsweetened cocoa

1 large egg

1¾ cups all-purpose flour

1 teaspoon salt

¾ teaspoon baking soda

¾ cup semisweet chocolate chips

1 cup walnuts or pecans, chopped (optional)

Preheat oven to 375 degrees.

In a large bowl, cream butter and sugar until light and fluffy. Beat in milk and vanilla. Beat in cocoa, egg, flour, salt, and baking soda. Stir in chocolate chips. Add walnuts or pecans (if using).

Drop by rounded tablespoon on a cookie sheet 3 inches apart. Bake for 9 minutes. Let cool on cookie sheet for a few minutes, then transfer to racks to cool completely.

Makes about 4 dozen cookies.

STORY

MY VERY CLOSE FRIEND AND business partner, Linda, was married to a wonderful man named George. He worked as a contractor for most of his life, and began cooking in his early fifties with the same attention to detail as his finish carpentry. For years, he tried out cookie recipes and tested them on us over the holidays. He made these particular love cookies for Linda at their outdoor July Fourth party. She has a passion for chocolate but hates nuts so he designed these cookies with her in mind. He did, however, sneak a few nuts in a quarter batch just for me because he knew how much I love them.

The last time I saw him he was very ill. Linda walked into the room, George turned to me, and said, "All she has to do is walk into a room and I'm flooded with warmth and happiness."

I thought how lucky they both were.

After he died, George's granddaughter made a book of his recipes, which she gave to his family and close friends. That first holiday season, I made a double batch of George's Love Cookies and sent them, along with a few dozen cookies from the Christmas cookie party, to Linda. As I made them, I tried to add additional love, the love that George always put in these cookies.

Lemon Drops

1 large egg

1 teaspoon grated lemon zest

1½ teaspoons fresh lemon juice

4½ ounces nondairy frozen whipped topping, thawed

1 package lemon cake mix

½ cup confectioners' sugar, sifted

Preheat oven to 350 degrees.

In a large bowl, beat egg. Add lemon zest and juice. Stir in whipped topping and cake mix and mix well.

Drop by teaspoon into confectioners' sugar. Coat well.

Place on a well-greased cookie sheet and bake for 12 minutes. Transfer cookies to racks to cool.

Makes 4 to 5 dozen cookies.

Crispy Chocolate Jumbles

1¼ cups all-purpose flour

½ teaspoon baking soda

¼ to ⅛ teaspoon salt

8 tablespoons (1 stick) unsalted butter, softened

1 cup sugar

1 large egg

1 teaspoon pure vanilla extract

2 cups Rice Krispies

2 cups semisweet chocolate chips

½ cup chopped dried cranberries or cherries (you can add or
substitute nuts or banana chips for the dried fruit)

Preheat oven to 350 degrees.

In a medium bowl, sift together flour, baking soda, and salt. Set aside. In a large bowl, beat butter and sugar together with mixer on medium speed until creamy, about 3 minutes. Add egg and vanilla and beat until blended.

Stir flour mixture, cereal, chocolate chips, and dried cranberries into butter just until mixed.

Drop dough by tablespoonfuls on a lightly greased cookie sheet. Bake for 12 minutes, until golden. Transfer to a wire rack to cool.

Makes about 6 dozen cookies.

Chocolate-Dipped Coconut Macaroons

5⅓ cups (14 ounces) flaked sweetened coconut

⅔ cup sugar

6 tablespoons all-purpose flour

¼ teaspoon salt

4 egg whites

1 teaspoon almond extract

1 package (8 ounces) semisweet baking chocolate, melted

Preheat oven to 325 degrees.

In a large bowl, mix coconut, sugar, flour, and salt. Stir in egg whites and almond extract until well blended. Drop by tablespoonfuls onto parchment paper–lined cookie sheet.

Bake for 20 minutes or until edges of cookies are golden brown. Immediately transfer cookies to wire racks to cool completely.

Dip cookies halfway into melted chocolate. Let stand at room temperature or refrigerate on wax paper–lined tray for 30 minutes or until chocolate is firm. Store in tightly covered container up to 1 week.

Makes about 3 dozen cookies.

Chocolate Chip Kisses

CHEWY AND FULL OF COCONUT AND CHOCOLATE CHIPS!

2⅔ cups (7 ounces) shredded sweetened coconut

⅔ cup sweetened condensed milk

1 teaspoon pure vanilla extract

1 cup (6 ounces) semisweet chocolate chips

Preheat oven to 350 degrees. Line cookie sheets with parchment or wax paper.

In a medium bowl, combine coconut, condensed milk, and vanilla. Stir in chips. Drop by well-rounded teaspoon onto cookie sheets.

Bake for 10 to 12 minutes or until edges are lightly browned. Cool before removing from cookie sheets.

Makes about 3 dozen 2-inch cookies.

MOLDED OR HAND-FORMED COOKIES

Molasses Sugar Cookies

(MARYBETH'S MOMS FAVORITE COOKIE)

12 tablespoons (1½ sticks) unsalted butter

1 cup sugar

¼ cup molasses

1 large egg

2 cups sifted all-purpose flour

2 teaspoons baking soda

1 teaspoon ground cinnamon

½ teaspoon ground cloves

½ teaspoon salt

Preheat oven to 375 degrees.

Melt butter in 3-or 4-quart saucepan over low heat. Allow to cool. Pour melted butter into a large bowl and add sugar, molasses, and egg. Beat well.

In a medium bowl, sift together flour, baking soda, cinnamon, cloves, and salt. Add to butter mixture. Mix well and chill thoroughly. Form into 1-inch balls and roll in sugar. Place 2 inches apart on a greased cookie sheet. Bake for 8 to 10 minutes. Transfer to a wire rack to cool. Makes about 4 dozen cookies.

STORY—THE GREAT MOLASSES COOKIE BAKE-OFF

WE WERE GATHERING COOKIE RECIPES to be included in this book and Ann commented, "I have a great molasses cookie recipe from my grandmother."

"Well, I have one from my mom written in her own handwriting!" Marybeth fished out the card, one of those precious relics from our foremothers.

One of us suggested a bake-off. Here's the story of a cookie and the bake-off:

This is one of those memories that is laced with food, a specific memory of my grandmother, who I called Lala, and me baking these cookies. I had two children, both still in diapers, when she came to visit me in Michigan. I was 30, she was 80. Unknown to either of us at that time, cancer was gathering its cruel claws and she would be dead two years later. It would be her only visit to my home.

She had come to impart womanly wisdom to me, and she sprinkled advice as we enjoyed our time together. I remember her suggestions about child rearing, landscaping my garden, and keeping myself absolutely neat, dressed, and made-up as I was now the role model for a little girl who would learn how to be a woman by watching me.

Lala was a fabulous cook. Her father had been a German-trained baker, and she worked in the family bakery making meat turnovers and pies, which she sold from her wagon to steel workers on work breaks. In charge of her own kitchen, she made every meal special. Cooking was one of her passions.

During her visit, she taught me how to make an apple tart and these molasses cookies. As we were making them, she commented, "One of the important things you should do as a mother is to have homemade cookies ready for your children. Remember my cookie canister?"

"Of course." Lala's cookies filled a ceramic container in the shape of a fat woman, holding a wooden spoon and smiling with great glee.

"Keep it filled so you can give your children something homemade and wonderful when they come home from school, one of those emblems that say home and caring and love."

At that time, I was working in a child guidance clinic, raising two children, and trying to grow, freeze, and can all our vegetables. I've thought about Lala's advice throughout the years. It seemed I could better give to my children by reading them stories, and taking them to swimming, soccer games (yes I was a soccer, football, field hockey, and lacrosse mom), plays, and concerts. The cookies that were baked we usually baked together, and entailed gobs of dough and colorful icing on fingers, cheeks, counters, and floors.

I remembered all this as I mixed Lala's molasses cookies for the bake-off, which we held on a warm, rainy July night at a birthday party for a friend. When our cookies were out of the oven we lay them side by side on the table. Our cookies looked very different. Marybeth's were perfectly formed, smaller, and lighter in color. Mine were dark, flat, and lumpy with walnuts. We asked people to taste them and give comments. Mine were crispier. Hers had extra spices in them (cinnamon and cloves). Mine tasted more molasses-y. Hers were chewier. It really was like comparing apples and pears.

Two recipes, both with the same name. Both delicious. A case of different strokes for different folks. Take your pick.

Lala's Molasses Cookies

16 tablespoons (2 sticks) unsalted butter, softened

¾ cup sugar

1 large egg

1½ cups all-purpose flour

¾ teaspoon baking soda

Pinch of salt

⅓ cup molasses

¾ cup chopped walnuts

Preheat oven to 350 degrees.

In a large bowl, cream butter and sugar. Beat in egg until light.

In a medium bowl, sift flour, baking soda, and salt. Add flour mixture to butter mixture alternately with the molasses. Add walnuts.

Drop by teaspoon 2 inches apart on a cookie sheet. Bake for about 15 minutes. Transfer cookies to racks to cool.

Makes about 4 dozen cookies.

Peanut Butter Crinkles

16 tablespoons (2 sticks) unsalted butter

1 cup creamy peanut butter

1 cup granulated sugar

1 cup firmly packed light brown sugar

2 large eggs

1 teaspoon pure vanilla extract

2½ cups all-purpose flour

1 teaspoon baking powder

1 teaspoon baking soda

1 teaspoon salt

1 large bag Hershey Kisses (removed from wrappers)

Preheat oven to 375 degrees.

In a large bowl, mix first 6 ingredients at medium speed. Add flour, baking powder, baking soda, and salt. Shape into ¾-inch balls and roll in sugar (small is better for kisses).

Place balls 2 inches apart on ungreased cookie sheet and bake for 12 to 15 minutes. Immediately press a chocolate kiss into each cookie while still on cookie sheet, then transfer to racks to cool.

Makes about 6 dozen cookies.

Almond Cookies

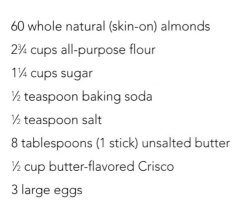

60 whole natural (skin-on) almonds

2¾ cups all-purpose flour

1¼ cups sugar

½ teaspoon baking soda

½ teaspoon salt

8 tablespoons (1 stick) unsalted butter

½ cup butter-flavored Crisco

3 large eggs

3 teaspoons almond extract

To blanch almonds, put them in boiling water until the skins crinkle. You can test this by taking one out, running it under cool water, and seeing if the nut can be easily removed from its skin. Drain the almonds and let cool, then remove skins.

Preheat oven to 350 degrees. Roast almonds on a rimmed baking sheet until light brown. Watch them very closely so they do not burn.

Leave oven on but turn down to 325 degrees.

In a large bowl, combine flour, sugar, baking soda, and salt.

Cut in butter and Crisco with a pastry blender until mixture resembles cornmeal. Add 2 of the eggs and the almond extract and mix. The mixture will be crumbly.

Roll dough into 1-inch balls. Set them on a cookie sheet lined with parchment paper. Place an almond on top of each ball and press down to flatten. Beat remaining egg with a little water and brush on top of each cookie. Bake for 15 to 18 minutes. Transfer cookies to a rack to cool. They are even yummier the next day.

Makes 5 dozen cookies.

Peanut Butter & Chocolate Sandwiches

PEANUT BUTTER COOKIES

2½ cups creamy peanut butter

1½ cups firmly packed light brown sugar

1 teaspoon baking soda

2 large eggs

2 teaspoons pure vanilla extract

All-purpose flour, for shaping

CHOCOLATE FILLING

10 ounces bittersweet or semisweet chocolate, coarsely chopped
(2 cups)

8 tablespoons (1 stick) unsalted butter, cut into 4 pieces

To make the cookies: Position a rack in the center of the oven and preheat oven to 350 degrees. Line 4 cookie sheets with parchment or nonstick baking liners.

Using a stand mixer fitted with the paddle attachment, beat peanut butter, brown sugar, and baking soda on medium speed until well blended, about 1 minute. Add eggs and vanilla and mix on low speed until just blended.

Shape level tablespoons of the dough into 1-inch balls. (The dough balls may be frozen for a month. Thaw overnight in the refrigerator before proceeding with the recipe.) Arrange balls 1½ inches apart on the cookie sheets. Using a lightly floured glass or measuring cup, press down lightly on the balls. Bake one sheet at a time for 10 to 11 minutes, until the cookies are puffed and crackled but still moist looking. Transfer the cookie sheet to a rack to cool, about 10 minutes.

To make the filling: Melt chocolate and butter in a microwave or in a medium heatproof bowl set in a skillet with 1 inch of barely simmering water, stirring with a rubber spatula until smooth. Remove from the heat and set aside, stirring occasionally, until cool and slightly thickened, 20 to 30 minutes.

To assemble the sandwiches: Turn half of the cooled cookies flat side up. Spoon 2 teaspoons of chocolate filling onto the center of each cookie. Top with remaining cookies, flat side down. Press gently on each cookie to spread filling almost to the edge. Set on a rack until filling is firm, 20 to 30 minutes.

Makes about 30 sandwich cookies (or 60 single cookies).

Hazelnut Shortbread Sticks

1 cup all-purpose flour

½ teaspoon baking powder

¼ teaspoon salt

8 tablespoons (1 stick) unsalted butter, softened

⅓ cup sugar

½ cup finely ground skinned toasted hazelnuts plus ⅓ cup coarsely
   chopped skinned toasted hazelnuts

1 teaspoon pure vanilla extract

4 ounces high-quality milk chocolate, chopped

Position rack in center of oven and preheat to 325 degrees. Line
large cookie sheet with parchment paper.

In a medium bowl, whisk flour, baking powder, and salt to
blend. Set aside. Using electric mixer, beat butter and sugar in a
large bowl until smooth. Beat in the ½ cup finely ground hazelnuts
and vanilla. Beat in flour mixture until just combined.

Shape dough by tablespoons into 3-inch logs. Place on
cookie sheet, spacing 1 inch apart. Bake for about 20 minutes

until light golden brown around edges. Cool on cookie sheet for 5 minutes, then transfer to rack to cool completely.

Stir milk chocolate in top of double boiler over barely simmering water until melted and smooth. Remove from over water. Place the ⅓ cup coarsely chopped hazelnuts in a small bowl. Dip one end of each cookie into the melted chocolate, then into the coarsely chopped hazelnuts. Let stand until chocolate is set, about 1 hour.

Store in an airtight container at room temperature.

Makes about 20 cookies.

TIP: If you can't find skinned hazelnuts, here is a method you can use to skin them. Preheat oven to 350 degrees. Spread nuts on a rimmed baking sheet and toast for 12 to 15 minutes, until skins darken. Wrap the toasted hazelnuts in a thin kitchen towel and rub together. The skins will rub off. To grind toasted hazelnuts, put them in a food processor and pulse. Do not overprocess or you will end up with hazelnut butter.

Chocolate Thumbprints

Almond Cookie Dough

½ cup granulated sugar

½ teaspoon salt

¾ cup whole almonds

12 tablespoons (1½ sticks) unsalted butter, cut into large chunks
and slightly softened

4 teaspoons pure vanilla extract

¼ teaspoon pure almond extract

3 cups all-purpose flour

Chocolate Thumbprints

⅓ of a batch (10½ to 11 ounces or 1¼ cups) freshly made Almond
Cookie Dough (above)

¼ cup coarse sugar (such as turbinado, Demerara, or sanding
sugar)

2½ ounces bittersweet or semisweet chocolate, coarsely chopped

5 teaspoons unsalted butter, softened

To make the almond cookie dough: Process granulated sugar and salt in a food processor until it looks powdery and a little finer, 30 to 60 seconds. Add almonds and process until they are finely chopped, about 20 seconds. Add butter and vanilla and almond extracts. Pulse until butter is smooth, scraping bowl as necessary. Add flour and pulse until soft dough begins to form around blade. Transfer dough to a large bowl and stir briefly with a rubber spatula to be sure it is evenly mixed. Portion dough into equal thirds. If you have a scale, weigh each third; each should weigh 10½ to 11 ounces. (If only making one batch of Chocolate Thumbprints, wrap and refrigerate two-thirds of the Almond Cookie Dough.)

To make the Chocolate Thumbprints: Scoop up a generous teaspoon (2 level teaspoons) of the dough and shape it into a 1-inch ball with your hands. Roll ball in the coarse sugar and set it on a tray lined with wax paper. Repeat with the rest of dough, setting balls slightly apart. Press a thumb or forefinger, dipped in flour, into each ball to create a depression. Cover and refrigerate cookies for at least 2 hours, but preferably overnight.

Position a rack in center of oven and preheat oven to 325 degrees.

Remove cookies from refrigerator and arrange them 1 inch apart on an ungreased or foil-lined cookie sheet. Let cookies warm to room temperature before placing in oven. Bake cookies for 10 minutes. Gently redefine depressions with tip of a wooden spoon's handle, if necessary. Rotate sheet and continue to bake for 8 to 12 minutes, or until tops are lightly colored and bottoms are golden brown. Transfer to a rack to cool.

While cookies cool, prepare filling. Put the chocolate and butter in a heatproof bowl set in a wide skillet of almost simmering water, or in top of a double boiler. (Or microwave on medium power for 1 to 2 minutes, stirring after first minute.) When chocolate is almost completely melted, remove bowl from heat and stir until completely melted and smooth. Spoon filling into each depression. If filling hardens while using, reheat it in pan of hot water.

Makes about 2 dozen cookies.

Mexican Wedding Cakes

1 cup confectioners' sugar

16 tablespoons (2 sticks) unsalted butter, softened

2 teaspoons pure vanilla extract

2 cups all-purpose flour

1 cup finely chopped almonds, pecans, or walnuts

¼ teaspoon salt

Preheat oven to 325 degrees.

In a large bowl, combine ½ cup of the confectioners' sugar, the butter, and vanilla and beat until light and fluffy. Add flour, almonds, and salt. Mix until dough forms.

Shape dough into 1-inch balls. Place 1 inch apart on ungreased cookie sheets. Bake for 15 to 20 minutes, or until set but not brown. Immediately remove from cookie sheets. Cool slightly, then roll in the remaining ½ cup confectioners' sugar. Transfer to a rack to cool completely. Reroll in confectioners' sugar.

Makes about 5 dozen cookies.

TIP: Many recipes call for butter that is softened or at room temperature. It is important to bring to room temperature (around 70 to 75 degrees). The consistency of the dough will be completely different if used directly from the refrigerator. If you are creaming sugar with cold butter, it will not dissolve evenly and you can end up with crystals in your dough. When softened, it will be a rich, creamy texture that is ideal for making yummy cookies. If you need to soften quickly, put the butter in the microwave for a few seconds.

Peanut Butter Balls

1¼ pounds confectioners' sugar

16 tablespoons (2 sticks) unsalted butter, softened

1½ cups creamy peanut butter

6 ounces semisweet chocolate chips

⅓ bar paraffin wax

In a stand mixer fixed with a paddle attachment, mix sugar, butter, and peanut butter together. Roll into balls.

Melt chocolate chips and paraffin wax in a double boiler. Dip balls in chocolate and place on wax paper.

Makes about 4 dozen 1-inch balls.

TIP: There are a few fundamental guidelines to successfully melting chocolate:

Make sure the chocolate is chopped into uniform pieces. Never try to melt large bars or blocks of chocolate that have not been chopped.

Avoid all contact with water! Make sure your bowls, workstation, and spatulas are completely dry.

Melt the chocolate slowly over low heat. Chocolate is very delicate and can become lumpy or grainy if overheated.

Stir the chocolate frequently with a rubber spatula.

Chocolate retains its shape when melted, so the only way to know if it is truly melted is to stir it. Do not rely on appearances alone.

REFRIGERATOR COOKIES (SLICE & BAKE)

Freeze them in ice
And dance a square
Bake them here
And eat them there![2]

[2] Beilenson, Edna, *Holiday Cookies* (New York: Peter Pauper Press, 1954).

Basic Refrigerator Cookies

¾ cup granulated sugar

¾ cup firmly packed light brown sugar

16 tablespoons (2 sticks) unsalted butter, softened

1½ teaspoons pure vanilla extract

2 large eggs

3 cups all-purpose flour

1½ teaspoons baking powder

¾ teaspoon salt

1 cup finely chopped walnuts or pecans

In a large bowl, combine sugars, butter, vanilla, and eggs and beat well. Add flour, baking powder, and salt and blend well. Stir in nuts. Divide dough into three equal parts. Shape each into a roll 1½ inches in diameter. Wrap each roll in plastic wrap and refrigerate for 2 hours or until firm.

Preheat oven to 425 degrees. Cut dough into ¼-inch slices. Place slices 1 inch apart on ungreased cookie sheets.

Bake for 5 to 7 minutes, or until light golden brown. Immediately transfer cookies to a rack to cool.

Makes about 7 dozen cookies.

TIP: For flavored cookies, add 1 tablespoon grated lemon or orange zest to flour.

Orange Pistachio Slices

2¼ cups all-purpose flour

1 teaspoon baking soda

1 teaspoon cream of tartar

16 tablespoons (2 sticks) unsalted butter, softened

1½ cups sifted confectioners' sugar

1 large egg

½ teaspoon orange extract

4 teaspoons grated orange zest

1½ cups dried cherries, finely chopped

½ cup chopped pistachios

1 cup melted white chocolate

In a medium bowl, stir together flour, baking soda, and cream of tartar. Set aside.

In a large mixing bowl, beat butter and sugar until fluffy. Add egg and orange flavoring. Stir in orange zest, cherries, and pistachios. Add flour mixture and stir until well blended.

Shape dough into two 11-inch rolls (2½-inch-diameter). Wrap in plastic and chill in the freezer for 2 hours.

Preheat oven to 375 degrees. Cut rolls into ¼-inch slices and place 2 inches apart on a greased cookie sheet. Bake for 8 to 10 minutes. Transfer to wire racks to cool. Decorate with strips of melted white chocolate.

Makes about 6 dozen cookies.

Ultimate Double Chocolate Cookies

1 bag (11.5 ounces) 60% cacao bittersweet chocolate chips

6 tablespoons (¾ stick) unsalted butter, softened

3 large eggs

1 cup sugar

⅓ cup all-purpose flour

½ teaspoon baking powder

12 ounces semisweet chocolate chips

1 cup chopped walnuts

In double boiler over hot water, melt bittersweet chocolate chips and butter. In a large bowl, beat eggs and sugar with an electric mixer until thick. Stir in chocolate mixture. Set aside.

In a small bowl, stir together flour and baking powder. Stir into chocolate mixture. Gently mix in semisweet chocolate chips and walnuts (dough will be gooey). Refrigerate for 30 minutes to firm up.

On a sheet of plastic wrap, form chilled dough into 2 logs,

each 2 inches in diameter and 8 inches long, and wrap tightly. Refrigerate at least 2 hours or until firm.

Preheat oven to 375 degrees. With sharp knife, cut logs into ¾-inch slices and place on greased or parchment-lined cookie sheet.

Bake for 14 minutes or until shiny crust forms. Cookies should still be soft inside. Transfer cookies to a rack to cool.

Makes 2 dozen cookies.

Chocolate-Nut Wafers

2 cups all-purpose flour

½ cup unsweetened cocoa (not Dutch-process)

½ teaspoon ground cinnamon

16 tablespoons (2 sticks) unsalted butter, softened

2⅔ cups confectioners' sugar

¾ teaspoon salt

1 large egg

2 cups chopped walnuts

1 cup chopped pistachios

In a medium bowl, whisk flour, cocoa, and cinnamon together. Set aside.

Using a stand mixer fitted with paddle attachment (or in a large bowl using a hand mixer), cream butter on medium speed until soft and creamy but not melted. Add confectioners' sugar and salt. Mix on medium-low speed until thoroughly combined (about 5 minutes) scraping bowl as needed. Reduce speed to low and add egg. Mix until blended.

Add walnuts, pistachios, and flour mixture. As soon as dough comes together, stop mixer. Scrape dough onto a large sheet of plastic wrap. Using the wrap to help shape dough, gently press it into a 6-inch square 1½ inches thick. Wrap in plastic and refrigerate until firm enough to slice (at least 4 hours).

Preheat oven to 400 degrees. Line a cookie sheet with parchment. Unwrap dough, trim edges, and slice square into four 3 x 3 x 1½-inch squares. With a sharp knife, slice each square ⅛ to ¼ inch thick. Lay the cookies ½ inch apart on cookie sheet.

Bake cookies for 8 to 10 minutes, rotating sheet halfway through, until tops look dry and nuts look golden. Let cookies cool on cookie sheet for about 10 minutes, then transfer to a rack to cool completely.

Makes about 12 dozen cookies.

Cranberry-Cherry Pinwheels

1½ cups unsweetened dried cranberries

1 cup cherry preserves

¼ cup water

1 teaspoon ground cinnamon, divided

3⅓ cups all-purpose flour

¾ teaspoon baking powder

⅛ teaspoon baking soda

½ teaspoon salt

4 tablespoons (½ stick) unsalted butter, softened

1¼ cups sugar

3 large egg whites

3 tablespoon corn or canola oil

2 tablespoons milk

2 teaspoons pure vanilla extract

1½ teaspoons finely grated orange zest

Combine cranberries, cherry preserves, water, and ½ teaspoon of the cinnamon in a medium saucepan. Simmer, stirring frequently, for 5 to 8 minutes, or until mixture is soft and most of the liquid is absorbed. If the mixture looks dry, stir in 1 tablespoon water. Transfer to a food processor and process until smooth. Cover and refrigerate until cool. (Filling may be stored up to 48 hours. Let return to room temperature and stir well before using.)

In a large bowl, whisk together flour, baking powder, baking soda, salt, and remaining ½ teaspoon cinnamon. Set aside. In a large bowl, with an electric mixer, beat together butter, sugar, egg whites, oil, milk, vanilla, and orange zest until well blended. Beat in half of the flour mixture until just incorporated. Stir in the remaining flour mixture until well blended. Divide dough in half. Form each half into a rough oblong shape about 6 inches long. Center each log on a 12-inch-long sheet of wax paper. Cover with a second 12-inch-long sheet of wax paper. Press, then use a rolling pin to roll each log into an even 11 x 9-inch square, occasionally checking the underside of the dough and smoothing any creases. Patch the dough as necessary to make the sides relatively straight. Keeping the wax paper in place, layer the rolled dough on a tray and refrigerate until fairly firm, at least 30 minutes. Dough may be held up to 24 hours; warm up slightly before using.

Working with one square of dough at a time (leave the other in the refrigerator), peel away and discard top sheet of wax paper. Spread half the filling evenly over entire surface of dough; filling layer will be thin. Peeling off second sheet of wax paper as you work, tightly roll up dough jelly-roll style. Gently stretch out log center slightly to yield an even roll. Wrap roll in wax paper, twisting ends to prevent unrolling. Place on a tray or cookie sheet. Repeat with remaining dough. Freeze for 2½ hours or until rolls are firm enough to cut neatly.

Preheat oven to 375 degrees. Generously coat several cookie

sheets with nonstick spray. Using a large, sharp knife, cut rolls crosswise into scant ¼-inch slices. With a wide spatula, transfer the pinwheels to the cookie sheets, spacing about 1½ inches apart.

Bake in upper third of oven for 10 to 13 minutes or until edges are browned and tops are lightly colored. Rotate sheets halfway through baking for even browning. Immediately transfer cookies to wire racks to cool. Store in an airtight container in refrigerator for 10 days or in the freezer for up to 1 month.

Makes about 5 dozen cookies.

Nut-Edged Lemon Slices

Cookies

   ¾ cup granulated sugar, divided

   ¾ cup firmly packed brown sugar

   16 tablespoons (2 sticks) unsalted butter, softened

   1½ teaspoons pure vanilla extract

   2 large eggs, one separated

   3 cups all-purpose flour

   1 tablespoon grated lemon zest

   1½ teaspoons baking powder

   ¾ teaspoon salt

   ¾ cup finely chopped walnuts or pecans

Icing

   1¼ cups confectioners' sugar

   5 teaspoons fresh lemon juice

   1 drop food coloring (red or green at holiday time; yellow is nice, too)

To make the cookies: In a large bowl, combine ½ cup of the granulated sugar, the brown sugar, butter, vanilla, whole egg and egg yolk; beat well. (Refrigerate remaining egg white.) Add flour, lemon zest, baking powder, and salt; mix well. Divide dough into 3 equal parts on 3 sheets of wax paper. Shape each into roll 1½ inches in diameter. Wrap; refrigerate 1 hour or until firm.

Preheat oven to 400 degrees. Lightly grease cookie sheets. In a small bowl, combine nuts and remaining ¼ cup granulated sugar. Slightly beat the egg white. Brush chilled dough with egg white, then roll in nut mixture, pressing nuts firmly into dough. Cut dough into ¼-inch slices. Place slices 1 inch apart on cookie sheets.

Bake for 5 to 7 minutes or until light golden brown. Immediately transfer cookies to rack to cool.

To make the icing: Blend confectioners' sugar, lemon juice, and food coloring together in a medium bowl until smooth.

Drizzle the cookies with lemon icing.

Makes about 7 dozen cookies.

TIP: Cookie dough can be frozen for up to 6 weeks. Slice and bake frozen dough as directed above.

ROLLED COOKIES (CUTOUTS)

Just keep your head,
Be nimble & quick,
And rolling out cookies
Is really no trick![3]

---

[3] Beilenson, Edna, *Holiday Cookies* (New York: Peter Pauper Press, 1954).

Santa Faces

Cookies

1½ cups sugar

1 cup shortening or 8 tablespoons (1 stick) unsalted butter

2 teaspoons pure vanilla or lemon extract

3 medium or large eggs

4½ cups sifted all-purpose flour

1 teaspoon baking soda

½ teaspoon salt

Glaze

2 cups confectioners' sugar

2–3 tablespoons milk (½ teaspoon lemon or vanilla extract is optional)

To make the cookies: Preheat oven to 350 degrees. Lightly grease a cookie sheet.

In a large bowl, cream sugar, shortening, vanilla or lemon

extract, and eggs together. In a large bowl, sift flour, baking soda, and salt together, then beat in to the sugar mixture.

Roll dough very thin (no thicker than ⅛ inch) on a lightly floured surface. Cut out shapes using a Santa face cookie cutter; turn cutter upside down and work dough into the cutter to shape features (keeping fingers away from the edge). Tap edge of cutter and cookie will flop out onto greased cookie sheet. Bake for 7 to 8 minutes. Transfer cookies to rack to cool completely.

To make the glaze: Mix confectioners' sugar and milk. Lightly frost faces. Decorate with colorful sugars to make the cookies resemble a Santa face.

Makes about 3 dozen cookies.

Sugar Cookies

Cookies

4 cups all-purpose flour

1 teaspoon baking powder

½ teaspoon salt

16 tablespoons (2 sticks) unsalted butter, softened

2 cups granulated sugar

2 large eggs

2 teaspoons fresh lemon juice

Grated zest of 2 lemons (or 2 teaspoons pure vanilla extract)

Royal Icing

2 large egg whites, at room temperature

1 pound confectioners' sugar

Juice of 1 lemon

Food coloring as needed

To make the cookies: In a large bowl, sift together flour, baking powder, and salt. Set aside.

Using a stand mixer fitted with the paddle attachment, cream butter and granulated sugar until fluffy. Beat in eggs. Add flour mixture and mix on low until combined.

Stir in lemon juice and zest (or vanilla, if preferred). Wrap dough in plastic and chill for 1 hour.

On floured surface, roll out dough ⅛ inch thick. Cut into shapes. Transfer to ungreased cookie sheet and chill until firm, about 30 minutes.

Preheat oven to 325 degrees.

Bake for 8 to 10 minutes or until edges start to brown.

Transfer cookies to racks to cool.

To make the royal icing: using a stand mixer fitted with paddle attachment, combine egg whites and confectioners' sugar on low speed. Stir in lemon juice until spreadable. Add food coloring.

Use immediately to decorate the sugar cookies or store in airtight container.

Using your creative talents, you can decorate the cookies with colorful sugars and let dry completely.

Makes about 4 dozen cookies.

Raspberry Linzer Cookies

THE LITTLE WINDOW IN THIS NUT-FLAVORED COOKIE REVEALS A DELICIOUS FRUIT FILLING

½ cup sliced almonds

½ cup coarsely chopped hazelnuts

2 cups plus 1 tablespoon all-purpose flour

¾ cup sugar

2 teaspoons grated lemon zest

½ teaspoon baking powder

½ teaspoon salt

½ teaspoon ground cinnamon

¼ teaspoon ground cloves

14 tablespoons cold unsalted butter

1 large egg

1 tablespoon cold water

½ cup raspberry preserves

Confectioners' sugar, for dusting

In a food processor, grind the almonds and hazelnuts with ½ cup of the flour until finely textured but not powdered.

Add remaining 1½ cups plus 1 tablespoon flour, the sugar, lemon zest, baking powder, salt, cinnamon, and cloves. Pulse to combine. Cut butter into ½-inch cubes and add to flour mixture; pulse until mixture looks like coarse meal. Do not overprocess. Transfer mixture to a large bowl. Whisk egg and water together in a small bowl, sprinkle over flour mixture, and toss gently to combine. Dough should hold together when pinched. (If it seems dry, sprinkle on a bit more water.) Gather dough into 2 balls and knead briefly just to blend. Wrap in plastic and chill until firm, 2 to 3 hours.

Preheat oven to 325 degrees. Line several cookie sheets with parchment. Generously flour a work surface. Roll one ball of the dough ³⁄₁₆-inch thick. (Keep second ball in refrigerator and, if dough warms up to point of being sticky while you are working with it, return to refrigerator.) Cut out as many 2½-inch rounds (or other shapes) as possible, rerolling scraps to make more rounds. Arrange on cookie sheets about ¾ inch apart. Cut 1¼-inch holes (or other shapes) in center of half the rounds. Reroll these center scraps to make more cookies. Bake for 15 minutes, or until edges are lightly browned. Let cool on cookie sheets. Repeat with remaining dough.

To assemble, spread a heaping ½ teaspoon preserves on underside of whole cookie rounds. Dust confectioners' sugar over the perforated cookies and place them on top of the whole cookies, bottom sides against the preserves.

Makes about 32 2½-inch sandwich cookies.

Chocolate-Dipped Espresso Shortbread

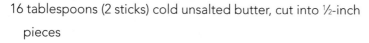

16 tablespoons (2 sticks) cold unsalted butter, cut into ½-inch
  pieces

½ cup sugar

½ teaspoon salt

2¼ cups all-purpose flour

2 tablespoons finely ground espresso beans

9 ounces semisweet chocolate, chopped

1 tablespoon vegetable shortening

Using a stand mixer fitted with the paddle attachment, beat the butter, sugar, and salt on low speed until butter combines with sugar but isn't perfectly smooth, 1 to 2 minutes.

Add flour and ground espresso and mix on low speed, scraping the bowl frequently until dough has just about pulled together, about 3 minutes. Don't overmix.

On a lightly floured surface, roll dough to about ¼ inch thick. Aim for a uniform thickness to ensure even baking. Cut dough into bars or squares with a sharp knife or, using cookie cutters, cut out shapes as close to one another as possible. Reroll scraps together and cut out more cookies. If the dough becomes sticky, refrigerate it briefly.

Position racks in the upper and lower thirds of the oven and preheat to 300 degrees. Arrange cookies on 2 parchment-lined cookie sheets and refrigerate until chilled, at least 20 minutes. Bake cookies for 30 minutes to 1 hour, or until golden on the bottom and edges and pale to golden on top. Halfway through baking time, rotate cookie sheets and swap their positions for even baking. If cookies are done before 30 minutes, reduce oven temperature to 275 degrees for remaining batches. If they take longer than 1 hour, increase temperature to 325 degrees.

Set a sheet of parchment or wax paper on a work surface. Put the chocolate and shortening in a small heatproof bowl and set the bowl over a pan of simmering water. Melt chocolate, stirring until it is smooth. Dip half of each cookie into chocolate. Set cookies on parchment and let chocolate set up at room temperature, about 2 hours.

Makes about 7 dozen 1½-inch heart-shaped cookies.

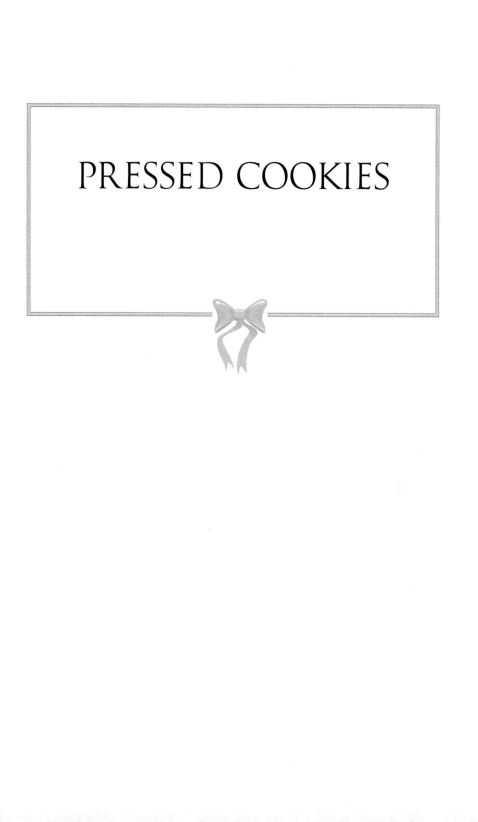

PRESSED COOKIES

$\mathcal{P}izzelle$

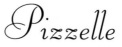

12 large eggs

3 cups sugar

1 pound (4 sticks) unsalted butter, melted and cooled (or Imperial margarine, not light)

7 to 8 cups all-purpose flour

8 teaspoons baking powder

4 teaspoons pure vanilla extract

2 teaspoons anise extract (or lemon or orange extract)

Confectioners' sugar, for decorating

Using a stand mixer, beat eggs until smooth. Add sugar and mix well. Add cooled butter and continue to blend. While mixer is running on low, lightly whisk flour and baking powder together. Turn off mixer and add dry ingredients on a low speed until well mixed. Add the vanilla extract and anise (or whichever extract you decide to use). Turn up mixer and blend until smooth. If it's too thick you can add another egg; if too thin add a couple table-spoons flour and mix again.

Heat up a pizzelle iron. Light indicates when the iron is ready.

Place a heaping teaspoon of batter in center of waffle pattern, close iron, and count to 20 or 25. You want pizzelles to be very lightly browned. Remove pizzelles from iron immediately and cool on racks. Sprinkle both sides with confectioners' sugar. So beautiful to look at and so yummy to eat!

Makes about 10 dozen pizzelles.

STORY—PIZZELLE TRADITIONS

IT IS GENERALLY BELIEVED THAT pizzelles originated in a middle region of Italy in ancient times, and were made to mark an annual celebration. Initially baked over an open fire with relatively simple but effective irons, the early pizzelles often were proudly embossed with the family crest or some hint of the village of origin.

Over time it became tradition to use pizzelles to celebrate any holiday or festive occasion, and eventually there were pizzelles for everyone at Christmas and Easter. The modern patterns found on these delicious waffle cookies most commonly are floral on one side and a basket-weave pattern on the other.

The recent increased popularity of pizzelles is the result of greater recognition of their delicious versatility. For example, pizzelles, when still hot, can be formed into cylinders, cones, and mini-baskets that can hold a wide variety of delicious fillings for festive occasions. The range of taste experiences that can be created with fillings of formed pizzelles is virtually endless.

Pistachio Meringues with Toasted Coconut

¾ cup confectioners' sugar

½ cup superfine sugar

Pinch of salt

4 large egg whites

½ teaspoon cream of tartar

¼ teaspoon pure vanilla extract

⅓ cup unsalted pistachios, chopped medium fine, plus
   3 tablespoons finely chopped pistachios for garnish (optional)

⅓ cup shredded unsweetened coconut, lighted toasted

Position racks in upper and lower thirds of oven. Preheat oven to 175 degrees. Line a large heavy cookie sheet with parchment.

Sift together confectioners' sugar, superfine sugar, and salt. Using a stand mixer fitted with the whisk attachment (or in a large bowl with a hand mixer), beat egg whites and cream of tartar. Begin mixing on medium-low speed until frothy. Increase speed to medium-high and beat until whites form soft peaks. Continue beating while gradually sprinkling in sifted sugars. When all sugar is added, increase speed to high and whip until firm, glossy peaks form. Add vanilla and ⅓ cup pistachios and beat until just blended, about 10 minutes.

Spoon about half of the meringue into a large pastry bag fitted with a large (#8) star tip. Pipe shapes as you like onto prepared cookie sheet about ½ inch apart. For kisses, about 1½ inches wide and about 2 inches from tip to base. If the tip gets clogged with a nut, use the back of a small knife or spoon to pry open the points of the star tip slightly and the nut will wriggle out. Sprinkle the toasted coconut over the meringues along with a dusting of finely chopped pistachios, if you like.

Bake meringues for 3 hours or until dried and crisp but not browned. Turn off oven (leave door shut) and let meringues sit in the oven for about 1 hour. Remove from oven and gently lift off parchment. Serve immediately or store in an airtight container up to 1 month.

Makes about 40 meringues.

Cream Cheese Spritz Cookies

16 tablespoons (2 sticks) unsalted butter, softened

3 ounces cream cheese, softened

1 cup sugar

1 large egg, separated

1 teaspoon pure vanilla extract

2½ cups all-purpose flour, sifted

Colored sugars or other decoration, for sprinkling (optional)

Position a rack in center of oven and preheat oven to 375 degrees.

Using a stand mixer fitted with the paddle attachment (or in a large bowl using a hand mixer), beat butter, cream cheese, and sugar on medium speed until light and fluffy, about 4 minutes. Add egg yolk and vanilla and beat again until blended. Add flour and mix on low speed until blended.

Fit a cookie press with a die plate. Scoop up about one-fourth of dough and, using a small amount of flour if needed, shape dough into a log just narrower than barrel of cookie press. Slide log into cookie press and spritz cookies directly onto ungreased cookie sheets about 1 inch apart.

Lightly beat egg white and brush tops of cookies. Sprinkle with colored sugar or other decorations (if using). Repeat with remaining dough.

Bake for 10 to 12 minutes, or until cookies are just golden around the edges. It is best to bake one sheet at a time. Let cookies cool on cookie sheet on a rack for 5 minutes before transferring them to a rack to cool completely. Store at room temperature or freeze in an airtight container, separating cookie layers with wax paper.

Makes about 100 cookies, depending on the size and style.

Vanilla Malted Cookies

2¾ cups all-purpose flour

¾ cup plain malted-milk powder

1 teaspoon baking powder

¾ teaspoon salt

16 tablespoons (2 sticks) unsalted butter, softened

3 ounces cream cheese, softened

1 cup sugar

1 vanilla bean, split, seeds scraped and reserved

1 large egg

½ teaspoon pure vanilla extract

Preheat oven to 350 degrees. Line a cookie sheet with parchment paper.

Whisk together flour, malted-milk powder, baking powder, and salt. In a bowl, with an electric mixer, beat butter and cream cheese on medium speed until creamy. Mix in sugar and vanilla seeds (reserve pod for another use). Add egg and vanilla extract, and combine. Reduce speed to low. Add flour mixture and mix until just combined.

Transfer dough to a pastry bag fitted with a large star tip (such as Ateco #825). Pipe 2½-inch-long strips onto cookie sheet, spacing them about 1 inch apart. Bake for 11 to 15 minutes, until bottom edges are golden brown. Transfer cookies to a rack to cool. Cookies can be stored in airtight containers up to 1 week.

Makes about 6½ dozen cookies.

BAR COOKIES

Play a Bar
And dance a square
Bake them here
And eat them there.[4]

---

[4] Beilenson, Edna, *Holiday Cookies* (New York: Peter Pauper Press, 1954).

Seven-Layer Bars

8 tablespoons (1 stick) unsalted butter or margarine

1½ cups graham cracker crumbs

1 can (14-ounces) sweetened condensed milk

1 cup butterscotch-flavored chips

1 cup semisweet chocolate chips

1⅓ cups flaked unsweetened coconut

1 cup chopped pecans or walnuts

Preheat oven to 350 degrees (325 degrees for glass dish).

In a 13 x 9-inch baking pan, melt butter in oven. Sprinkle crumbs over butter. Pour sweetened condensed milk evenly over crumbs. Top with remaining ingredients in order listed. Press down firmly.

Bake for 25 minutes or until lightly browned. Cool.

Chill, if desired. Cut into bars. Store covered at room temperature.

Makes 2 to 3 dozen bars.

TIP: Line entire pan with a sheet of aluminum foil first. When bars are baked, cool; lift up edges of foil to remove from pan. Cut into individual squares. Lift off of foil.

Brown Butter Hazelnut Shortbread with Fleur de Sel

Adapted from America's Dairy Farmers. Browning a portion of the butter before adding it to the batter intensifies the buttery taste of this crisp, nutty shortbread. The final flourish of fleur de sel (sea salt) enhances the flavors and textures of the cookie by adding a salty edge and satisfying crunch.

Shortbread

> 16 tablespoons (2 sticks) unsalted butter, softened but still cool
>
> ½ cup granulated sugar
>
> ½ cup lightly packed light brown sugar
>
> ¼ teaspoon plus a pinch of salt
>
> 1 large egg, separated
>
> 1½ teaspoons pure vanilla extract
>
> 2 cups all-purpose flour

Topping

1½ cups chopped hazelnuts

2 tablespoons granulated sugar

½ teaspoon ground cinnamon

½ teaspoon ground nutmeg

1 heaping teaspoon coarse fleur de sel (sea salt)

6 ounces bittersweet chocolate (at least 60% cacao)

To make the shortbread: Place ½ stick of butter (4 tablespoons) in small saucepan over medium heat. Melt and cook until butter stops foaming, smells toasty, and begins to brown, about 10 minutes. The browner the butter, the deeper the flavor, but do not let it blacken or burn. Set aside to cool to room temperature.

In a large bowl, with an electric mixer, beat remaining 1½ sticks butter until creamy. Add the sugars and ¼ teaspoon of the salt and continue to beat until light and fluffy. Add egg yolk, vanilla, and cooled, browned butter. Mix to combine. Then add flour, 1 cup at a time, and stir with a wooden spoon to combine. Chill dough for 20 to 30 minutes.

Preheat oven to 350 degrees with oven rack in the middle. Butter a 15 x 10-inch jelly-roll pan. Divide dough into 8 rough portions and arrange them evenly in pan. Press dough into an even layer to fill pan. In a small bowl, beat egg white with a pinch of salt. Brush mixture evenly over dough.

For the topping: Sprinkle hazelnuts over the top of the shortbread and press down lightly. In a small bowl, combine sugar with cinnamon and nutmeg and sprinkle over nuts. Sprinkle sea salt over top.

Bake for 25 minutes, rotating pan once halfway through

baking, until golden brown and crisp. Cool for 10 minutes and cut into 1½-inch squares or diamonds. Transfer to a rack to cool.

Melt chocolate in a metal bowl set over a pan of simmering water. Drizzle over shortbread.

Makes about 5 dozen.

Hazelnut Shortbread Sticks

1 cup all-purpose flour

½ teaspoon baking powder

¼ teaspoon salt

8 tablespoons (1 stick) unsalted butter, softened

⅓ cup sugar

½ cup finely ground skinned toasted hazelnuts plus ⅓ cup coarsely
   chopped skinned toasted hazelnuts

1 teaspoon pure vanilla extract

4 ounces high-quality milk chocolate (such as Lindt), chopped

Position rack in center of oven and preheat to 325 degrees. Line
large cookie sheet with parchment paper.

Whisk flour, baking powder, and salt in medium bowl to blend.
In a large bowl, with an electric mixer, beat butter and sugar until
smooth. Beat in ½ cup finely ground hazelnuts and vanilla. Beat
in flour mixture until just combined.

Shape dough by tablespoon into 3-inch logs. Place on cookie
sheet, spacing 1 inch apart. Bake cookies for about 20 minutes
or until light golden brown around edges. Cool on cookie

sheet for 5 minutes, then transfer to rack to cool completely.

Stir milk chocolate in top of double boiler over barely simmering water until melted and smooth. Remove from over water. Place ⅓ cup coarsely chopped hazelnuts in small bowl. Dip one end of cookie into melted chocolate, then into coarsely chopped hazelnuts. Repeat with remaining cookies. Let stand until chocolate is set, about 1 hour. Store in airtight container at room temperature.

Makes about 20 cookies.

FIVE

Candy

Every woman's secret sin and passion

Mary's Famous Peanut Brittle

2 cups sugar

1 cup light corn syrup

½ cup water

1 teaspoon unsalted butter

2 cups raw peanuts

1½ teaspoons pure vanilla extract

1½ teaspoons baking soda

Butter a jelly-roll pan or rimmed baking sheet. Mix sugar, corn syrup, and water in a large, heavy pan. Dissolve over low heat. Increase heat and cook to Soft Ball stage (230 degrees on a candy thermometer). Add butter and peanuts and cook until syrup turns golden brown (300 degrees). Remove from heat and add vanilla and baking soda. Stir until it foams well. Pour into jelly-roll pan. Let set until cooled, then turn pan over and let brittle fall out of pan (you may have to wiggle the pan for brittle to release). Leave brittle out of pan for a couple of hours and break into pieces and ENJOY!!

TIP: A candy thermometer is a thermometer used to measure the temperature and therefore the stage of a cooking sugar solution. It is a *must* for making candy. These thermometers can also be used to measure hot oil for deep frying.

There are several kinds of candy thermometers available. These include traditional liquid thermometers, coil spring "dial" thermometers, and digital thermometers. The digital thermometers tend to read the temperature more quickly and accurately, and some models have an alarm when the thermometer hits a certain temperature. Many models have markers for the various stages of sugar cooking.

Cook the candy as directed. Some recipes will give you a temperature to aim for, while others may use one of the following terms: "thread," "soft ball," "medium ball," "firm ball," "hard ball," "very hard ball," "light (or soft) crack," "hard crack," or "caramelized sugar" stages. The temperatures for some or most of these terms should be indicated on your candy thermometer. Place the candy thermometer in the pan with the cooking candy. Be sure the bulb of the thermometer never touches the bottom of the pan, or the temperature will register too high. You want to find out the temperature of the candy mixture, not of the pan.

STORY

THIS IS SUCH A SPECIAL recipe for Marybeth's family (7 siblings!) and we all *love* peanut brittle. This is the story: Growing up, we literally spent hours shelling peanuts for our Mom to make our beloved candy. It was always the start of our holidays, and even on a tight budget she made it incredibly special. In our family, it wasn't about big expensive gifts, but all the love and spirit of the season. Mom would make several batches (hence the hours spent shelling peanuts!) and then poured the molten candy on our old-fashioned red Formica countertop to harden up. After about an hour, we would smash it into bite-size pieces and gobble it up immediately! You can now buy peeled raw peanuts, thank heavens. I have made this recipe for years, and have many peanut brittle junkies whose habit I happily support. I hope your family enjoys this wonderful candy as much as ours does!!

English Toffee

1 pound (4 sticks) unsalted butter

2 cups sugar

2 tablespoons light corn syrup

⅓ cup water

11½ ounces milk chocolate chips

1 cup finely chopped toasted nuts (almonds, pecans, or walnuts)

Line a 15 x 10 x 1-inch pan with foil, extending over edges. In a 3-quart saucepan, melt butter and stir in sugar, corn syrup, and water. Cook over medium-high heat to boiling, stirring until sugar is dissolved. Using a candy thermometer, cook over medium heat to Soft Crack stage, about 15 minutes. (Soft Crack is between 270 degrees and 290 degrees, but for this recipe I have found it best to stay at 290. At 270 degrees the toffee was too chewy and it will stick to your teeth!)

Pour into prepared pan and spread evenly. Cool 5 minutes or until top is just set. Sprinkle chocolate onto toffee. Spread evenly, then sprinkle with nuts. Press into chocolate and let cool for several hours. If necessary, place in fridge.

Holding foil, lift candy out of pan. Break into pieces. To store, layer candy into airtight containers between sheets of wax paper.

Oven Caramel Corn

2 cups firmly packed light brown sugar

16 tablespoons (2 sticks) unsalted butter, cut up

½ cup light corn syrup

1 teaspoon salt

1 teaspoon pure vanilla extract

½ teaspoon baking soda

6 to 8 quarts popped large-kernel popcorn

1 to 2 cups dry-roasted peanuts (optional)

Preheat oven to 250 degrees.

Place brown sugar, butter, corn syrup, and salt in a 2-quart pan and bring to boil. Boil for 5 minutes stirring constantly. Do not overboil.

Add vanilla and baking soda, stirring after each addition.

Put popcorn into 2 large foil pans and keep warm until you put caramel topping on it. You may add dry-roasted peanuts to popcorn before adding hot mixture.

Pour caramel mixture over popped corn covering all kernels.

Place pans in the oven and bake for 1 hour, stirring 3 or

4 times during baking to ensure that the popcorn is evenly coated.

Remove pans from oven, and place caramel corn on wax paper to separate and cool.

Store in cans or plastic bags.

Easy Chocolate-Covered Peanuts

1 bag (12-ounces) Reese's peanut butter chips
1 bag (6-ounces) semisweet chocolate chips
2 cups salted dry-roasted peanuts

Melt all the chips together in a 3- to 4-quart saucepan over medium heat, stirring constantly. When melted, remove pan from heat. Stir in peanuts until coated. Drop by tablespoon onto a lightly greased cookie sheet (or use wax paper). Place in refrigerator for 5 to 10 minutes until firm. Store in a covered container.

Makes about 3 dozen.

Sugared Nuts

3 cups nuts (peanuts, whole almonds, pecan halves, or whatever
you prefer)

1 cup sugar

½ cup water

In a 12-inch skillet, bring nuts, sugar, and water to a boil over medium heat. Cook, stirring occasionally, until syrup has caramelized and the nuts are well coated, 12 to 15 minutes.

Preheat oven to 300 degrees. Butter a large rimmed baking sheet.

Immediately spread coated nuts onto baking sheet. Bake for 10 minutes; stir. Bake 10 minutes more; stir. Cool on a rack. Store in an airtight container.

Makes about 4 cups.

(For cinnamon sugared nuts, add ½ teaspoon ground cinnamon with sugar).

Candied Walnuts or Peanuts

1½ cups sugar

½ cup sour cream

1 teaspoon pure vanilla extract

1 pound walnut halves or peanuts

In a large saucepan, combine sugar and sour cream, and bring to a boil. Boil for 5 minutes. Remove from heat. Add vanilla and walnuts or peanuts. Stir until nuts are thoroughly coated. Spread and cool on wax paper.

Makes about 4 cups.

Mom's Friday Night Fudge

2 cups sugar

½ cup unsweetened cocoa

1 cup milk

3 tablespoons unsalted butter

1 teaspoon pure vanilla extract

In a medium saucepan, bring sugar, cocoa, and milk to a boil over medium-high heat. Increase heat to high and continue cooking until temperature reaches Soft Ball stage (238 degrees on a candy thermometer). Add the butter and vanilla. Using a whisk or wooden spoon, stir vigorously until well mixed and pour into a buttered 8- or 9-inch square pan.

Put pan in sink of cold water and beat until the fudge looks dull or starts to set up. Let cool and cut into 1-inch squares.

Makes 64 to 81 squares.

Chocolate-Dipped Caramels

1 cup sugar

16 tablespoons (2 sticks) unsalted butter

1 cup dark corn syrup

1 can (14 ounces) sweetened condensed milk

1 teaspoon pure vanilla extract

2½ cups semisweet chocolate chips

2 tablespoons shortening

Line an 8 x 8-inch baking dish with foil. Lightly grease the foil.

In a large saucepan, combine sugar, butter, and corn syrup and bring to a boil over medium heat. Cook for 7 minutes without stirring.

Stir in sweetened condensed milk and bring to a boil. Cook, stirring constantly, for 10 minutes or until a candy thermometer reaches 245 degrees.

Remove from heat and stir in vanilla. Pour into prepared baking dish. Let stand 8 hours at room temperature.

Cut the cooled caramel into ½-inch squares and shape into balls.

In a medium saucepan, melt chocolate and shortening over medium heat. Remove from heat.

Dip balls into melted chocolate mixture and place on wax paper. Chill 8 hours.

Makes about 10 dozen caramels.

Pecan Praline Morsels

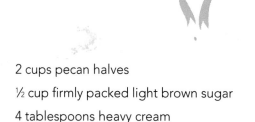

2 cups pecan halves

½ cup firmly packed light brown sugar

4 tablespoons heavy cream

Preheat oven to 350 degrees.

Combine all ingredients in a medium bowl and spread in 8-inch square baking pan sprayed with cooking spray. Bake for about 20 minutes or until the coating dry, stirring once. Remove from oven and cool. Stir once more. Store morsels in an airtight container.

Makes approximately 2 dozen morsels.

Chocolate Peanut Toffee

1 pound (4 sticks) unsalted butter, cut into pieces

2 cups sugar

¼ teaspoon salt

4 cups whole cocktail peanuts plus 1 cup chopped

7 to 8 ounces bittersweet chocolate (70% cacao), finely chopped

Grease a 15 x 10 x 1-inch jelly-roll pan or rimmed baking sheet and put on a heatproof surface.

In a 4- to 5-quart heavy pot, bring butter, sugar, and salt to a boil over medium-high heat, whisking until smooth. Boil, stirring occasionally, until mixture is deep golden and reaches Hard Crack stage (300 degrees on a candy thermometer), 15 to 20 minutes.

Immediately stir in whole peanuts, and then carefully pour hot toffee into center of prepared baking pan. Spread evenly with spatula, smoothing top, and let stand for 1 minute, then sprinkle chocolate on top.

Let stand until chocolate is melted, 4 to 5 minutes. Spread chocolate over toffee with cleaned spatula. Sprinkle evenly with chopped peanuts and freeze until chocolate is firm, about 30 minutes.

Remove pan from freezer, and break toffee into pieces.

Toffee keeps about 2 weeks layered between sheets of parchment paper in an airtight container at cool room temperature.

Makes about 3 pounds.

Truffles Without Trouble

3 cups semisweet chocolate chips

2 tablespoons unsalted butter, softened

1 cup heavy cream

Chopped nuts, confectioners' sugar, or unsweetened cocoa,
   for garnish (optional)

To make the filling: Place a heaping cup of the chocolate pieces
and the butter in a large bowl. Bring the cream to a simmer in a
small saucepan over low heat. Remove from heat and pour half
the cream into the bowl. As the chocolate melts, slowly whisk the
mixture together until smooth. Then gradually add the remaining
cream until it is completely incorporated and is thick and shiny.

To form the truffles: Pour mixture into a 2-inch-deep baking
pan, spread evenly, and place in the freezer for 30 minutes or
until set (it should have the consistency of fudge). Using a melon
baller or a small spoon, form rounds and place them on a baking
sheet lined with parchment or wax paper. Let the truffles harden
in the freezer for about 15 minutes. After removing from the
freezer, roll the truffles between your hands into marble-size

spheres, squeezing slightly (try to do this quickly, otherwise they will become too soft). You can now dust the truffles with cocoa and serve them as is, but they will hold their shape better if you coat them with chocolate first.

To make the coating: Make the chocolate glaze while the truffles are in the freezer. Place the remaining chocolate pieces in a large bowl over a saucepan of simmering water and stir occasionally until the chocolate is completely melted. Remove from heat and let cool at room temperature, stirring occasionally until the chocolate starts to set. Drop the truffles into the melted chocolate and retrieve them with a fork and hold until excess chocolate drips off. Garnish immediately, if desired.

To garnish: For a nut garnish, roll the freshly coated truffles in a shallow dish of chopped nuts. For a sugar or cocoa garnish, set the freshly coated truffles on a plate and sift the sugar or cocoa over them. Turn the truffles and sift again to cover completely.

To store, place the truffles on a lined baking sheet and allow them to set in the refrigerator for 5 minutes. Truffles will keep for about 2 weeks, chilled or at room temperature, when stored in a tightly sealed container.

Makes about 4 dozen truffles.

Peanut Butter Truffles

1 cup peanut butter, chunky or creamy

4 tablespoons unsalted butter, softened

12 ounces semisweet chocolate, cut into small pieces (2 cups), or
   semisweet chocolate chips

1 cup unsweetened cocoa

In a large bowl, combine the peanut butter and butter and mix well. Chill the peanut butter filling, form the truffles, and coat them following steps from the Truffles Without Trouble (page 145).

Makes about 4 dozen truffles.

SIX

Packaging

PRETTY IS AS PRETTY DOES

I LOVE PACKAGING! AS GOOD as your cookies are, it is the packaging that presents them. Before each cookie bitch brings out her cookies, we anticipate the bundles of love and can't wait to see how creative we all are. The great thing about ending up with twelve thoughtful, creative packages is that you can re-gift them to a family member, friend, coworker, manicurist, hairdresser, teacher, or whomever you'd like.

We have discovered a few tricks over the past twenty years that we have been doing this. We have fun inventing novel ways to present a dozen cookies. It's important to note the packages do not need to be expensive. In fact, many of our favorites have come from a dollar store. We've used simple baker's boxes with frilly ribbons. We've had cookies in Christmas tins. One of our ladies made gorgeous lemony star cookies and put them in brown paper boxes and tied them up with string—they were simple and stunning! Some have been rolled in Christmas kitchen towels and potholders. We've received cookies in small velvet purses. One of our ladies made cookies that looked like mini hamburgers and she went to McDonald's and got their paper bags to pack the cookies in—it was very cool! We look for a package that is unique yet affordable. We do *not* spend a lot of money. We have been known to borrow ideas from magazines, cookbooks, Martha Stewart, food shows, Williams-Sonoma catalogues—you get the idea. We have used ribbons, tissue paper, cellophane, and rubber stamps. One of us had plain brown sandwich bags and her friends' children decorated them with holiday rubber stamps using colorful inks and drew pictures on them with Magic Markers. They were precious. Packaging turns the cookies into gifts!

When you choose your packages, keep in mind a few basic suggestions. First, choose a package size that is based on your particular cookie. If you have a smaller cookie, you would not want to put it in too large of a container. Your cookies will look lost.

Also, keep in mind the texture of your cookie. If your cookies are decorated, for example, you may need them to lie flat and not stack one on top of the other. If you want to include an inner wrapping, such as tissue paper, make sure it will not stick to the cookie. One of my cookie ladies made these darling mini cheesecakes in pastry with cherry topping. A few problems arose though when she tried to stack them. By the time they got to the party, they had practically all shifted and many were smushed together. She was devastated! They still tasted great, though they did not look as beautiful as they could have. We were all very supportive and we all learned a big lesson.

Something else to consider is how long the cookies keep. Many cookies can be stored in the freezer for a couple of months (my favorite kind of cookie). A good example of this would be drop cookies or a simple slice and bake (like the Orange Pistachio Slices). Other cookies that have frosting or are rolled in confectioners' sugar will not freeze well, and are best stored in the refrigerator.

Something to keep in mind regarding storage of all your different cookies—you want to store similar cookies together. For example, you would not want to store a crisp, crunchy cookie with a soft hermit-style cookie. What happens? The crisp cookies become soft, too. So, just remember to store your crisp cookies together and your softer cookies together.

Here are some suggestions for your packages:

* Traditional cookie tins (round canisters, square, or oblong)

* Seasonal coffee mugs, preferably large

* Cellophane bags

* Paper bags

* Chinese takeout boxes, which can be decorated in many ways. One of us found some red silk ones for $1 each and she even bought a couple extra for her grandkids who used them as purses!

* Seasonal kitchen towels

* Holiday oven mitts or potholders

* Hobo-style fabric bags

* Wide-mouth canning jars

* Makeup bags

* Small, velvet purses

* Fabric bags

* Two-pound oatmeal boxes (these hold large round cookies beautifully)

* Plain white boxes with little see-through windows

* Cardboard boxes in a variety of shapes

* Freezer paper and bright, shiny ribbon

* Mini loaf pans

* Festive clay pots

* Gift bags (they come in all sizes and shapes)

THE POINT IS TO MAKE it fun. Make it an adventure. Be daring and creative. I personally have always loved to wrap presents, so this is right up my alley. Once you open your mind, the possibilities are endless. All the women love a package that can be used again, but they're extra fun when you can add a beautiful new coffee cup to your holiday collection, a new oven mitt, or a new dish towel. When you use it, you remember who gave it to you and which delicious cookies were so lovingly wrapped with it. That truly makes a special memory.

MAKEUP FOR COOKIES

Let's talk about "makeup" for your cookies, or going from plain to pretty. Some cookies are finished when the baking is done and they have cooled. They're ready to be placed in the packaging you have chosen and presented to the other cookie bitches. But I have baked many cookies that have needed an extra step to take them from plain to spectacular. And there are lots of ways we can do that.

One very simple way is to drizzle melted chocolate on the top of the cookie. I have used dark chocolate, white chocolate, and a combination with great success. When I start drizzling the chocolate, I use a toothpick to make squiggly designs and that works very well. You could also use a pastry bag with a small tip. Play around with the different tips and you will see how many possibilities there are.

Last year I made shortbread cookies shaped like small hearts. I flavored half the dough with fresh ground espresso beans and the other half with fresh lemon juice. When the cookies were baked, I dipped half of each heart in dark chocolate. And the fusion of espresso shortbread dipped in dark chocolate was exquisite. So was the lemon with a completely dissimilar flavor. Two entirely different tasting cookies in one batch. They were both delicious! It's so enjoyable experimenting with different combinations while offering variety to satisfy various tastes.

Thumbprint cookies are super fun to make because you can use so many fillings. Traditionally, the recipes call for some flavor of jam—apricot, raspberry, or orange marmalade. But you can use chocolate or caramel. Improvise and experiment. Put your own favorite tastes in them. Maybe minted chocolate or a chocolate/caramel swirl. Press a small peanut butter cup into the thumbprint—what a taste treat that would be! The sky is the limit!

The traditional holiday sugar cookie cutout is great fun to make and decorate. I have included a recipe in Chapter Four, so now let's think about all the ways to decorate our finished and cooled cookies. First make the frosting. You can use a royal icing. This icing becomes hard once it cools, so it works very well for holiday cookies. To make approximately 1½ cups of royal icing:

1 large egg white
¼ teaspoon fresh lemon juice
2 cups confectioners' sugar, sifted, plus extra as needed
Food coloring (optional)

In a small bowl, beat the egg white, lemon juice, and confectioners' sugar until mixture becomes stiff. You can add more confectioners' sugar if needed. Once the icing is the consistency you want, separate it into 2 or 3 smaller bowls, and, using a drop or two of food coloring, mix in the colors you want to use. You may want to leave some white.

If you are looking for an even simpler recipe, here's a basic powdered sugar icing recipe:

2 cups confectioners' sugar, sifted
½ teaspoon pure vanilla extract (you could also use lemon extract)

2 to 3 tablespoons milk or orange juice

Food coloring (optional)

Combine all ingredients in a small bowl, stirring in additional milk/orange juice as needed. Separate into smaller bowls and mix food coloring into icing for desired color.

Now that your cookies have cooled and your icing is at the perfect consistency, it is time to decorate! You can simply frost the cookies different colors. Or you can use paint brushes, toothpicks, and pastry bags to color parts of the cookie, make dots or stripes, pipe waves, or curls. You could dress a gingerbread man in blue overalls with a red shirt, and a gingerbread lady in a white dress with red polka dots.

There is a wide variety of items manufactured for baking decoration. I like colored sugars, which you can find in any color of the rainbow. Other decorations include the multicolored nonpareils and silver dragées (the beloved silver balls that hurt your teeth when you eat them, but that we love anyway). There is also a variety of sprinkles that come in a gazillion colors and shapes for any and all holidays.

Here is a small list of decorations you might have around the kitchen:

* Coconut (shredded and sweetened)

* Slivered almonds

* Variety of chopped nuts

* M&Ms (whole or chopped)

* Raisins

* Mini chocolate chips

This is a really fun activity to do with your kids, your husband, or your friends. You get ideas from one another and spur one another on. When you are finished you have a beautiful batch of individually decorated cookies. Take a picture and use it for next year's holiday card!

FINAL IMPORTANT TIP: Your beautifully decorated cookies must be completely cooled and the decorations set before going into the packaging. It could be quite disastrous if you package too soon. If you are layering cookies in a container, it is helpful to cut pieces of wax paper to fit in between the layers, which helps keep the goodies fresh, too!

All of the baking we do and all of the time we spend on adding the makeup to the cookies is paid back when we finally get together for the big night. We love to make delicious and beautiful cookies, but one of my dear cookie ladies could not have said it better: "It's not about the cookies, but rather about the people you love and who love you back!"

Yes, we spend a great deal of time baking and coming up with creative packaging ideas, but when we gather together to exchange our gifts, it's done with a lot of love and laughter. And the little disasters along the way—smushed-together cheesecakes, stuck caramel-frosted cookies, too-hard biscotti—just add to our time together and our book of memories.

SEVEN

Last-Minute Decorations and Food

A VERY IMPORTANT ELEMENT TO any party is the food. There are twelve of us and we all work. We have busy, full lives with barely enough time to get everything we need to accomplish done in a given day. Many of us come from work with maybe a stop at home to pick up our cookies. We come to the party hungry, so part of the fun is that each person brings an appetizer and a bottle of wine. Let's face it, twelve women and twelve bottles of wine without any food could make for a rather sloppy and *wild* party.

Each year, as the eve of the party arrives, I have the same feeling of anticipation. My house is lit with the holiday decorations that I have arranged with care and, of course, my Christmas tree is lit in the center of my living room.

And then the day arrives. I add the leaves to my table to make it large enough for all the yummy appetizers and food that will be arriving. I set out my festive plates and napkins and place candles all over the house for a warm and cozy atmosphere. Some years I have found fun paper plates and napkins that work well, too, so be creative! I pull down wineglasses and open the wine to let it breathe. I pick out the music that I will play—usually all my favorite holiday music to begin. I get the coffee pot ready for later, and set out the bowls for the soups that I make from scratch each year (recipes to follow). I want everything to be ready for the party because it becomes hectic once people arrive. Then, I want to focus on my guests as the party swings into motion.

As everyone begins to arrive, the level of excitement increases. Many of us haven't seen each other since the previous year's cookie party, so there are lots of exclamations and hugs and kisses as we all say our hellos. Each guest has her wine and appetizer or dish to share, and an armload or more of cookies in their glorious packages. We all beam with joy and excitement to see one another.

Once all the cookie ladies have arrived, the table is loaded with delicious food and we begin the feast. Because the dish or appetizer is something we have chosen to share and we often bring our favorites, there's a sense of family to the gathering. I never suggest what to bring and it works 100 percent of the time. We marvel at how talented we all are and, the fact is, we really are. We manage to juggle our jobs, our children, husbands/boyfriends, the occasional crisis, and still get cookies baked and packaged, food planned and prepared, and make it to the cookie party in style.

After the initial excitement of seeing one another and enjoying all our food, we find our way into the living room, or cookie party central. During all of this activity our token photographer (a guest who is not a cookie bitch) has been taking candid pictures of us, the food, the tree, and of course (dramatic music here) the cookies. The dressing room that holds the cookies waiting to be exchanged is truly a sight to behold. Close your eyes for a moment and imagine what 156 cookie packages, each containing a dozen delectable delightful cookies, might look like. It's truly an amazing spectacle. Every year I look at that collection and heave a big, happy sigh!

It's the culmination of many hours of mixing, stirring, and baking, all done with a hefty dose of love. What a blessing for this incredible group of women and a blessing for our chosen charity. It is what the holiday season is all about. This cookie exchange is the beginning of a holiday of sharing and giving. I cannot think of a better way to get it all going than with the style and finesse of this marvelous group of friends!

SO NOW FOR THE FOOD . . .

HERE'S A LIST OF STORE-BOUGHT appetizer items that have worked very well:

Fruit

Veggie tray

Hummus with pita bread

Cheese and crackers

Cold shrimp with cocktail sauce

Sushi

Guacamole and chips

Stuffed grape leaves

Poached salmon, chilled

Chicken wings

Deli food

Pistachios or cashews

Honey-roasted peanut butter with banana chips

Greek salad

Selection of olives

Chips and salsa

Assorted deli salads

I'm including several of our favorite recipes from over the years. I always request that my guests bring a favorite appetizer to share and I am never disappointed. The table is absolutely overflowing with countless delicious hors d'oeuvres and salads. These recipes represent a fine beginning to your party. Your guests will bring their own favorites each year and soon you will also have a fantastic selection of yummy appetizers, soups, and salads of your own.

Mild Guacamole

2 avocados, mashed

2 tablespoons finely minced onion

1 Roma tomato, seeded and chopped

1 clove garlic, minced

½ teaspoon salt

½ teaspoon ground cumin

1 tablespoon fresh lemon juice

Splash of Tabasco

Mix all of the ingredients in a medium bowl and let sit for a few hours. Taste and add more spice if you want.

Makes about 2 cups.

Bacon-Wrapped Dates

(DATILES CON BEICON)

4 Medjool dates

4 Marcona almonds, toasted

4 teaspoons Valdeón or Cabrales blue cheese

2 slices bacon, halved crosswise

Preheat oven to 400 degrees.

Cut each date along one side, removing the pit and replacing it with a Marcona almond. Place 1 teaspoon of cheese inside date and close it. Wrap each date with half a slice of bacon and secure it with a toothpick. Place on a small baking sheet and bake until golden brown.

Makes 4 servings.

Artichoke Dip

1 cup chopped scallions, white and light green parts only

1 cup grated Parmesan cheese

1 cup Hellman's Light Mayonnaise

1 can (14 ounces) artichoke hearts in water, chopped

Small deli rye bread or crackers, for serving

Preheat oven to 350 degrees.

Mix all ingredients in a large bowl. Spoon mixture into a covered casserole and bake for 30 minutes. Serve dip hot, with small deli rye bread or a variety of crackers.

Makes about 3 cups.

Pear Salad with Walnuts & Goat Cheese

½ pound mixed salad greens

1 large pear, peeled, halved, cored, and sliced

¼ cup balsamic vinaigrette

1 ounce crumbled goat cheese

¼ cup chopped walnuts

In a salad bowl, combine greens and pear. Add vinaigrette and toss lightly to coat. Sprinkle salad with cheese, toss, and top with walnuts.

Makes 2 servings.

TIP: When making this for a crowd, it is easy to triple or quadruple the recipe.

Brie en Croûte

1 sheet frozen puff pastry

1 tablespoon unsalted butter

½ cup walnuts or pecans

⅛ teaspoon ground cinnamon

8-ounce wheel of Brie

¼ cup firmly packed light brown sugar

1 large egg, beaten

Fresh baguette, sliced, for serving

Preheat oven to 375 degrees.

Defrost puff pastry for 15 to 20 minutes and unfold.

In a medium saucepan, melt butter over medium heat. Add nuts and sauté until golden brown, about 5 minutes. Add cinnamon and stir until nuts are well coated.

Place nut mixture on top of Brie and sprinkle brown sugar over mixture. Lay puff pastry on a flat surface and place Brie in center. Gather up edges of the pastry and press around Brie, gathering it at the top. Gently squeeze together excess dough and tie together with a piece of kitchen twine. Brush beaten egg over top and sides of Brie. Place Brie on a cookie sheet and bake for 20 minutes, or until pastry is golden brown.

Makes about 2 cups.

TIP: To give it a special look, cut extra pastry into heart or flower shapes and bake until golden brown and place around edges of Brie.

Crab Rounds

8 ounces cream cheese, softened

1 tablespoon milk

2 teaspoons Worcestershire sauce

2 tablespoons finely chopped scallions

¼ to ½ teaspoon cayenne pepper

½ cup shredded sharp Cheddar cheese

2 cans (3¼ ounces each) crabmeat

French bread, cut into ¼-inch slices

Preheat broiler.

In a medium bowl, with an electric mixer, whip cream cheese, milk, Worcestershire, scallions, and cayenne together. Fold in Cheddar to blend, and then fold in crabmeat. Toast both sides of French bread slices. Top with crabmeat mixture, sprinkle on more cayenne, and broil. Watch closely under the broiler, it only takes 1 or 2 minutes.

Makes about 2 dozen.

Green Chili Quiche

9-to 10-inch pie shell, chilled, then blind-baked

1½ cups shredded Monterey jack cheese

1 cup shredded Cheddar cheese

1 can (4 ounces) chopped green chilies

3 large eggs, slightly beaten

1 cup half-and-half

¼ teaspoon salt

¼ teaspoon ground cumin

Preheat oven to 350 degrees.

Sprinkle all jack cheese and ½ cup of the Cheddar over baked pie shell and spread chilies over cheese.

In a medium bowl, beat together eggs, half-and-half, salt, and cumin. Pour mixture over chilies and top with remaining ½ cup Cheddar cheese.

Bake for 45 minutes, or until center is set.

Makes 6 to 8 servings.

Ninh Hoa Grilled Meatballs

1 pound ground pork

5 cloves garlic, minced

1½ tablespoons sugar

1 teaspoon cornstarch

1½ teaspoons potato starch

½ teaspoon freshly ground pepper

1 tablespoon bottled fish sauce (*nuoc nam*)

Vegetable oil, for rolling meatballs

2 small heads Boston lettuce, leaves separated

Nuoc Cham Dipping Sauce (recipe follows)

In a medium bowl, mix together pork, garlic, sugar, cornstarch, potato starch, pepper, and fish sauce. Marinate, covered, in refrigerator for at least 2 hours.

Preheat a grill or broiler. With oiled hands, make 21 meatballs each 1 inch in diameter. If grilling, place 3 meatballs on each of 7 presoaked bamboo skewers. If broiling, place on a baking sheet or broiler pan. Grill or broil until meatballs are deep brown and crisp on all sides, about 3 minutes per side. Remove from skewers.

Serve the hot meatballs with lettuce leaves and dipping sauce. Makes 4 to 6 servings.

Nuoc Cham Dipping Sauce

1 to 2 small fresh red chilies, minced, or 1 to 2 teaspoons red pepper
  flakes

1 tablespoon white vinegar, heated

½ cup bottled fish sauce (*nuoc nam*)

¼ cup fresh lime juice

1 small carrot, shredded, rinsed, and squeezed dry

2 cloves garlic, minced

½ cup sugar

1½ cups warm water (just from the tap to touch)

Put the chilies in a medium bowl with vinegar. (If using flakes, soak them in vinegar for about 2 minutes.)

Add fish sauce, lime juice, carrot, garlic, and sugar to the chilies. Stir in water to dissolve.

Serve at room temperature. The sauce can be refrigerated for up to 3 days.

Makes about 2½ cups.

Roasted Carrot Ginger Soup

Roasting vegetables brings out all their natural sugars and intensifies flavors. By baking all the ingredients together, you'll get the best-tasting soup.

1½ pounds carrots, peeled and halved lengthwise

1 pound parsnips, peeled and quartered lengthwise

1 large sweet onion, sliced

3-inch piece fresh ginger, peeled and chopped

6 tablespoons unsalted butter

3 tablespoons dark brown sugar

8 cups rich chicken broth, plus more if needed

Pinch of cayenne pepper

Salt to taste

¼ cup crème fraîche, for garnish

Snipped fresh chives, for garnish

Preheat oven to 350 degrees.

Combine carrots, parsnips, onion, and ginger in a shallow roasting pan. Dot with butter and sprinkle with brown sugar. Pour cups of broth into pan. Cover well with aluminum foil and bake for 2 hours, or until vegetables are very tender.

Transfer vegetables and broth to a large soup pot. Add remaining 6 cups broth. Season with cayenne pepper and salt to taste. Bring to a boil, reduce heat, and simmer partially covered for 10 minutes.

Purée soup in a food processor, adding more broth if desired. Serve portions topped with a dollop of crème fraîche and a sprinkling of chives.

Makes ten ¾-cup servings.

Spicy Tomato Soup

1 tablespoon olive oil

1 tablespoon unsalted butter

1½ cups minced yellow onion

3 to 4 cloves garlic, minced or crushed

1 teaspoon dried dill (or more to taste) or 1 tablespoon fresh dill

½ teaspoon salt

Lots of freshly ground pepper

1 can (28 ounces) crushed tomatoes

2 cups chicken broth (or vegetable broth if you prefer)

1 tablespoon honey (optional)

1 tablespoon sour cream (low-fat is okay, too)

2 medium tomatoes, diced

Garnishes

Plain yogurt

Finely minced parsley and/or basil leaves

Finely minced scallions or chives

Heat olive oil and butter in a Dutch oven. Add onion, garlic, dill, salt, and pepper. Stir over medium heat for 5 to 8 minutes, or until the onions are translucent. Add canned tomatoes, broth, and optional honey. Cover and simmer over low heat for 20 to 30 minutes.

About 5 minutes before serving, whisk in sour cream, and stir in diced fresh tomatoes. Serve hot topped with the garnishes.

Makes four to six 1-cup servings.

Hungarian Mushroom Soup

2 to 4 tablespoons unsalted butter

2 cups chopped yellow onions

1½ to 2 pounds mushrooms, sliced

1 tablespoon tamari sauce

2 to 3 tablespoons minced fresh dill, or 2 to 3 teaspoons dried dill

1 tablespoon mild or spicy paprika

1 teaspoon salt

2 teaspoons fresh lemon juice

3 tablespoons all-purpose flour

2 cups chicken broth

1 cup milk (can be low-fat), at room temperature

Freshly ground pepper

½ cup sour cream (can be reduced-fat)

Finely minced fresh parsley, for garnish

Melt butter in a Dutch oven. Add onions and sauté over medium heat for 5 minutes. Add mushrooms, tamari, dill, paprika, and salt. Stir well and cover. Let soup cook for 15 more minutes, stirring occasionally. Stir in lemon juice.

Gradually sprinkle in flour, stirring constantly. Cook and stir another 5 minutes or so over medium-low heat. Add broth, cover, and cook for 10 minutes, stirring often.

Stir in milk and pepper to taste. Check to see if more salt is needed. Whisk in sour cream and heat gently. Don't boil or cook the soup after this point. Serve garnished with parsley.

Makes four to five ¾-cup servings.

Mandarin Orange Salad

1 can (10 ounces) mandarin orange segments, drained

1 tablespoon honey

½ teaspoon ground cinnamon

Handful of walnuts

Lettuce (romaine, red or green leaf, or mixed)

Olive oil

Salt and freshly ground pepper

Place mandarin orange segments in a bowl. Add honey and sprinkle with cinnamon. Set aside for several hours (or longer).

Toast walnuts in a 350-degree oven for about 5 minutes. Cool.

Wash and tear lettuce into bite-size pieces. Add enough olive oil to wet greens and toss well. Season with a little salt and pepper and sprinkle with walnuts.

Note: If taking to a potluck, wait to toss with olive oil and keep walnuts in a small bag until ready to serve.

Makes 4 servings.

Sweet Brie

1 cup firmly packed light brown sugar

¾ cup slivered almonds, toasted

2 tablespoons Scotch whiskey

1 tablespoon honey

2-pound wheel of Brie (about 8 inches)

Sliced French bread or assorted crackers, for serving

Preheat oven to 550 degrees.

In a small bowl, combine brown sugar, almonds, whiskey, and honey.

Place Brie in a shallow serving dish. Cover with almond mixture.

Bake for 4 to 8 minutes, or until sugar bubbles and melts and Brie is warmed through.

Reheat in microwave as needed.

Makes 2 cups.

EIGHT

Paaarty!!!

WE'VE REACHED THAT MOMENT in the party that we've been anticipating. We've spent time together and caught up on the details of each other's lives. We've had two or three glasses of wine and snacked for an hour or so. We're relaxed and pleasantly sated . . . not too full but just enough to give us that warm and cozy feeling. There's a moment when I know that it's time, usually one and a half to two hours into the party. Maybe it's a slight lull in the action around the table, quieter conversations, and a few gravitate toward the living room to claim their chairs for the night . . . for that cookie night at least. Every year we choose a different seat and settle in for the rest of the festivities. Maybe it's because we want to finish a conversation with a friend, or sit next to a different or favorite cookie bitch. Once we're in our seats, we stay and I make the anticipated announcement, "Let's do cookies!" We are all excited to taste everyone's cookies and see the gorgeous packaging. There's always that one "special" package that we all *ooh* and *aah* over, that packaging that someone finds that is truly unique.

This part of the party truly offers the most shining moments each year. Being part of this cookie exchange makes "us" important and what we "do" important. Cooking and making pretty presents really are important women's work, and not to be taken for granted. Throughout history, in cultures all over the world, women have gathered together to do the tasks that they are responsible for. Over the years women gathered in groups to sew and make clothing or items for the home. They would get together for child-rearing and together figure out the problems of the day. It was often the task of women to gather the food, take care of the home, and keep the fires burning—in other words, it is our heartfelt duty to make our homes into safe, comfortable havens for our families and for ourselves. Remember, our cookie club had its roots in my divorce. Families of whatever kind, typical and unconventional, involve the preparing and eating of food and the gathering together to share it. We are still doing those same things today and this cookie party is proof of that. The longer that this party is in existence, the stronger the bond is between these women. We gather together to share our baking tips and skills and to help one another to make our holiday time a little easier for our efforts that come to fruition this night. But it's more than that. We gather together to memorialize each other and our lives. We have formed a new family.

Once we're all settled, there is always a discussion about who wants to go first. Usually someone volunteers to be the first one. Among the women there are those who are more anxious about their cookies or packaging (although it's always totally perfect each and every year!). Another decision to be made is who will be in charge of the charity bag. And if someone happens to be absent, but has sent her cookies on ahead, someone needs to agree to collect her goodies. The first few minutes are spent just getting situated and organized for the exchange to begin.

These days the whole cookie process appears to be seamless, but it really took us several years to learn what works best for us. You most likely will have your own set of rules that are best for you and your friends. I love to hear about other cookie exchanges and how they work. There are many ways to make your party unique and special . . . I say just do it and it will come together on its own.

Finally, the first cookie bitch begins. We each have our very own moment of stardom, actually more like 10 minutes of stardom, and do we ever love it! As a group we focus on that one woman, what she says, and what she has to offer that year. If anything major has happened during the year, we'll hear about it during the cookie story. Sometimes it's a sad story and we are supportive; and sometimes it's joyful and we celebrate and applaud our friend. This is extremely important. Because each woman gets to tell a story, and because it is inevitably emblematic of the year and of her, we get to know each other deeply. For twenty years, we've heard one another's stories and witnessed one another's lives. We have survived so much together and, as a result, have become very close. We've heard about deaths, marriages, adoptions, children's problems, job promotions, marital problems, and joys. We have cried together and we have laughed together and this is what makes these women so unique. There are no rules about how long a woman talks. Somehow it always has worked out.

One year, I was battling cancer and although I was still undergoing chemotherapy and radiation it was very important to me that the cookie party happen right on schedule. I felt that my life was out of my control in so many ways and I needed the cookie party more than ever that year. I was extremely fatigued and weak from treatment and, as a result, decided to make a cookie that I had made before with great success. I baked my tried and true Orange Pistachio Slices (page 89). A very dear friend and fellow cookie bitch came to my rescue on the day of the party. She arrived at my home early to help with the final touches on my cookies and packaged them all up for me. I could not have done it without her and I love her to pieces for helping me to make it happen that year.

Another beautiful and sad story took shape the year that the son of one of our dear cookie club members was killed in a tragic work accident. She was still grieving as the cookie party approached and didn't think she'd be able to rally and do what it takes to make the 13 dozen cookies. One of the other women offered to do the baking for her. This amazing woman not only planned and made her own 13 dozen cookies, she also planned and made her friend's 13 dozen cookies. She packaged everything up and brought 26 dozen cookies to the party. This incredible act of love and kindness made it possible for our beloved sister to attend the party that year. Needless to say, there were lots of tears and oodles of love and support. We all gathered around her and held her up. For her it was an eye-opening experience to see the profound love and understanding everyone had for her. It was a healing moment for all of us.

We each take our turn and talk about the cookie for that year and where we first saw the recipe. Maybe it truly is an old family favorite (my personal favorite) or maybe over the past year we saw a great cookie recipe in a favorite magazine or on one of the food shows that are so popular now. We talk about what ingredients are in the cookie; if it's chocolate, we always say "*mmmmmmmm*" in unison, and it's quite hilarious. We like to know if it contains fruit or nuts or if it's dipped in something yummy. And then there is always some story that goes along with the cookie that year. This is always the most fun part of our presentation. Over the years there have been some real disasters that we still laugh about. For example, one year one of the ladies made her cookies and brought all 13 dozen to the party and put them in the special room for all the cookies and she went on to enjoy her friends and the food. When it came time for her to pass out her cookies she was missing a bag. She knew she had brought enough and we spent several minutes going through everyone's stash to see if somehow one of the ladies received two bags of cookies. I had gotten a puppy several months prior and I happened to see him out of the corner of my eye. I noticed the tell-tale cookie crumbs on his cute little dog lips! On further investigation, we discovered that he had gone into the cookie room, snagged his own private bag, and carried them into another room of the house and was having a secret party of his own! I had to forfeit my dozen and was a little sad not to be getting those cookies that year. I keep my eye on him now and I think he figured out that all he needs to do is stay close to the women and he will probably get a bite or two of a cookie without getting in quite so much trouble!

Another year, we had "The Cat Who Ate the Cookies" saga. A cookie bitch was making a totally yummy double-dipped chocolate peanut butter cookie that took some real organizational skills. She baked all 156 cookies and had dipped then all in milk chocolate. After letting them set for about an hour, she dipped them again, this time in dark chocolate and put them in trays to completely set up before putting them in the packages . . . an absolute must. They were on her kitchen counters and her bar area and any place she could find room to let them finish setting up. Her naughty cat jumped on the counters and proceeded to lick every single cookie. She said there was actually a lick mark on all the cookies from her cat's sandpaper tongue. Needless to say, she wasn't exactly happy that she had to start all over again! She had to buy all new ingredients and everything. We laughed so hard some of us had tears in our eyes as she told us the story. Bless her heart for hanging in there though and remaking all the cookies

I stopped over at a friend's house one night when she happened to be baking her cookies. She was most definitely mixing and stirring and it was a sight to see! There was flour literally everywhere, including all over her. We laughed so hard about it and we would have had tears if we weren't in danger of forming paste in our eyes because of all the flour dust in the air!

While we tell the story of the cookie, we end up talking about the year. It happens naturally. For example, a recipe that is baked that year because it is the favorite cookie of a father-in-law who passed away. Or one that is fun to make with a child. That's what makes this exchange so special: we take care choosing our cookie and the packaging and we share our lives with our friends. When we are finished exchanging, we really have a collection of cookies to give others and a deeper understanding of our friends.

So as each cookie bitch stands and tells her story we marvel at how talented and skillful she is. Don't rush your cookie bakers—let them have their 10 or so minutes of glory. They deserve it after all. They have persevered in spite of their personal trials and tribulations to get the job done. I believe that this is really a labor of love for all of us and we are thrilled to the bottoms of our toes to be able to share what we have with our fellow cookie bitches.

When that first lady is finished telling her story, she hands out her cookies in a circle fashion so we all know we received them and then we move on to the next guest. The whole process starts over and it continues until everyone has passed out her cookies. Usually about halfway we stop—sort of like the seventh-inning stretch—and refill our wineglasses, maybe get a little more food, chitchat for a few minutes, and then we get right back to the job at hand. We finish going around the circle and when we are all finished, we applaud one another for another fine effort.

We have had some rather spectacular cookies over the years. Several years ago a fairly new cookie bitch decided to go the extra mile to wow us with her talents. She made 12 Christmas cookies trees! She saw a picture of a cookie tree in a magazine and thought to herself, "I can do that!" The first thing she did was track down a sugar cookie recipe to make cutouts. She searched and found a set of nesting stars and ended up with 6 stars starting small and gradually getting larger. Each tree was 12 cookies; 2 cookies apiece for each size star. As she baked the cookies, halfway through she pulled out the cookie sheets and using a jumbo straw, punched a hole in the center of the cookie and then continued to bake them the rest of the way. She repeated this process until she had enough cookies to make 12 trees . . . one for each of us! She then frosted each cookie using green icing and used sugar sprinkles to finish the decorating, and went to a craft store and bought quarter-inch dowels and thick cardboard to use as the bases. She covered the cardboard with red and green flannel and glued the dowel to the base. She then started placing the cookies using the largest ones on the bottom and staggering the star points as she went, building the 12 trees. For the top, she used a chocolate kiss and then sprinkled the whole tree with edible sparkles. She went to Pier One and found boxes that had the correct size bottom and were deep enough for the trees. She carefully placed each tree in a box lined with tissue and finished it off with ribbons and a bow on top. When we saw those trees we were absolutely stunned. That tree is in the cookie party history books for sure! A few of us sprayed shellac to seal the tree and I still have it with my holiday decorations. It still amazes me that someone would go to such lengths to give us that beautiful gift. It demonstrates just how committed we all are to the success of this party and how much love and effort go into our cookies. I'm not sure if we'll see another star cookie tree, but I expect that there will be another cookie project that will make it to the Top Ten Cookies from the last nineteen years of baking.

Every year, I have someone take notes during the exchange and write down what each friend's cookie was, the story that goes along with it, and any humorous comments. Believe me, we're a hilarious group so there are numerous funny comments throughout the evening. Often, there's so much talking and laughing, we have to stop and get people to settle down for the next presentation. We want to hear what each of us has to say, but, at the same time, there are delightful side conversations. This collection of yearly stories makes fun reading and we are transported to cookie parties past.

By the time we have all presented our cookies, we are ready to stretch our legs and move around a bit. We usually continue to visit with our friends and know that another great cookie party is coming to an end. We hate to see the end of the night come and so we linger. This is where we change the holiday music to something more soulful, like Al Green. His music has been another tradition that we stick with every year and this year will be no different. We start to party and dance with each other and the tone of the party is relaxed and easy. The work is done and it's time to let our hair down and get silly, which we are experts at doing. We mix and mingle for maybe another 30 minutes or so and then the exits begin. The good-byes begin with promises to call soon and stay in touch. There have been years that we have had bunches of snow and I have had an overnight guest or two. Some come to this party from quite a distance and so they spend the night. Those are special years because we usually stay up late to talk and talk and talk—of course there is a lot of laughing going on too!

These are special times for us and I know that this party will continue far into the future until we can no longer muster up the strength to do all the baking. We'll figure it out then; maybe our children will take over for us, or our grandchildren. A niece or grandnephew. I don't have the rules for then but I'm sure as we approach that time, it will come to me and I will say "New Rule!"

There you have it! All the information you need to start your very own cookie exchange. Remember, it doesn't have to be just at the holidays, it can be anytime! Cookies are fun to make and share any time of the year. I have one final suggestion that I think will make your cookie party extra special. Start a scrapbook your very first year. Scrapbooking has become popular over the last few years, and I have seen beautiful scrapbook pages. I have made a few books myself as gifts. I took a class to learn the basic techniques for putting together a scrapbook and it has proven to be a great way to showcase a vacation or special event. Where I live, there are several stores that specialize in supplies and classes. Many have weekly workshops where you can continue a work in progress with the help of other classmates and experts!

I hope to present a finished album at our twentieth party for all of my cookie party attendees. We all know how much fun it is to review our high school yearbooks and photo albums. A scrapbook will have the same thrill. We have a good friend (who actually defected from being a cookie bitch!) who is a wonderful photographer. She takes candid shots and pictures of us as a group and of course we must all look youthful and gorgeous; needless to say, she has become an expert at Photoshop! I have collected all the pictures and, with the help of another cookie bitch, am making a scrapbook for all of us to share. As I have mentioned, I also have had someone take notes every year and I have years' worth of notes to type up and edit that will also go into the scrapbook. Finally, all the ladies bring me their recipes and I save them in a folder on my computer simple labeled "Cookie Party 2009" or "Cookie Party 2008"—you get the picture.

So here's my suggestion: Each year of your party, choose eight to ten of your best pictures and recipes and toss in the funny stories and comments and create two to three pages. It won't take long, and you will have a beautiful book to reminisce over. Just imagine what the book will look like in twenty years! Perhaps it's a project in which you all can share. Or each year choose a different person to be in charge of that year's pages. Or get a group organized and make it together. There is always fun to be had when friends get together for a joint project. Share your ideas—what you tried that worked and what didn't—on our website, www.christmas cookiecookbook.net. I can practically guarantee that you will have a blast. It will truly tell the story of your cookie party in years to come.

NINE

Baking Tips

1. **To sift or not to sift:** Pay attention to the wording of the recipe. If it says "1 cup sifted flour," you sift flour first and then measure. If the recipe says "1 cup flour, sifted" you measure first and then sift. If you need sifted flour but don't have a sifter, you can get by following these steps: 1) Stir flour with a fork 2) Dip measuring cup in flour and sweep off excess. Do *not* tamp down; the reason you sift is for lightness.

2. **How to make zest:** Zesting a lemon is getting the colored outer layer of the peel off, without taking the white part with it, which is called the pith. You don't want the pith, because it's bitter. You can buy a zester, which is a small tool with 4 holes. Wash the fruit to remove any pesticides and be sure it is completely dry for better zesting. You use the zester like a potato peeler and it makes long curly pieces. Some like to use a Microplane grater. Both are available any place kitchen gadgets are sold. If you don't want to go out

and buy a zesting tool, you can zest a lemon by running it over a cheese grater, or you can use a vegetable peeler on it; just peel off the outer layer without taking the pith with it, and then chop it finely, as you would mince garlic.

3. **Toasting nuts:** Preheat oven to 350 degrees. Scatter nuts on a rimmed baking sheet and toast for 5 to 10 minutes. The larger the nut, the longer the baking time. Toasting the nuts will make for a richer flavor. Check every 3 minutes and shake nuts. I sometimes rotate the baking sheet. Be careful not to scorch!!

4. **Confectioners' sugar:** A number of cookies are not complete without a final dusting of confectioners' sugar, also known as powdered sugar. Confectioners' sugar is actually granulated sugar that has been mechanically ground into a very fine powder. Put confectioners' sugar in a sifter and just tap the sides to sprinkle sugar over your cookies. This will lightly dust the cookies for that perfect sweet finish.

5. **Parchment paper:** Parchment paper is a natural high-density paper with a nonstick coating that can be used to line everything from cookie sheets to cake pans to muffin tins. Use parchment paper in the oven for nonstick results without the extra grease or spray. Cut and line your baking sheets and pans with either side of the parchment paper. Place food directly on the parchment paper—there is no need to add extra

spray or to grease the sheet of paper—and bake as directed. Treats will bake evenly and release from the paper with ease. Plus, because you're baking right on the paper, clean-up is a breeze. It really makes for more efficient baking. You can prepare one pan of cookies while one is baking. When you pull out the pan of cookies, slide off the sheet with cookies and slide the next sheet on and pop right back in the oven.

6. **Shortbread:** Shortbread is meant to be cooked slowly at low heat so it will often take an hour to bake. You want to bake it until the cookies crumble and fall apart. They will completely dry out and that is what you want. If you bake the shortbread just until set the shortbread will be very tender and crumbly. Baking 5 to 10 minutes longer will produce a firmer shortbread as it removes additional moisture and gives the shortbread a longer shelf life.

7. **Margarine vs. butter:** Butter is the result of beating cream (almost universally cow's cream) until all the fat coagulates. Butter is generally 80 percent fat, but it can range up to 85 percent. The remainder is water and milk solids. It is often salted. Margarine is an invention of man, and was originally based on beef fat, although now it is made of hydrogenated vegetable oils, some milk/water-based solution, vitamins A and D, and some flavoring and coloring agents. Like butter, it must consist of at least 80 percent fat. Nutritionally, margarine is a near-exact match for butter.

If affordable, opt for butter, and it is quite common to use unsalted butter when you're baking. If salted butter is what you have, using it will not significantly change the recipe.

Many recipes call for butter that is softened or at room temperature. It is important to bring to room temperature (around 70 to 75 degrees). The consistency will be completely different if used directly from the refrigerator. If you are creaming sugar with cold butter, it will not dissolve evenly and you can end up with crystals in your dough. When softened, it will be a rich, creamy texture that is ideal for making yummy cookies. If you need to soften quickly, put it in the microwave for a few seconds.

8. **Vanilla extract (or any extracts):**

Extracts—Diluted oils, usually containing about 20 percent pure oils and 80 percent additives. Alcohol is frequently used as an additive.

Flavors—When oil is not available for the flavor, natural and artificial flavors are used instead. Food-safe additives, possibly including alcohol, make up the bulk of the contents. Alcohol-free flavors must be used in the preparation of certain foods, like hard candies.

Pure extracts have a richer flavor. They may cost a bit more at the grocery, but it's worth the extra for a fullness of taste. Use the real deal if you can!

9. **Oatmeal:** Most recipes will call for old-fashioned rolled oats. Do not substitute quick one-minute oatmeal. Old-fashioned oatmeal is a larger cut and if you use the quick oats, which are cut much smaller, it completely changes the texture of the cookie. For example, in oatmeal cookies, old-fashioned oats will give you a chewier texture, and quick oats will taste more like you ground up the oats a bit, i.e., slightly less chew, with a more homogenous consistency.

10. **Baking soda and baking powder:** Both baking soda and baking powder are leavening agents, which means they are added to baked goods before cooking and cause them to rise. Baking powder contains baking soda, but the two substances are used under different conditions. Baking soda is pure sodium bicarbonate. When baking soda is combined with moisture the resulting chemical reaction produces bubbles of carbon dioxide that expand under oven temperatures, causing baked goods to rise. The reaction begins immediately upon mixing the ingredients, so you need to bake recipes that call for baking soda immediately, or else they will fall flat. Baking powder contains sodium bicarbonate, but it includes the acidifying agent already (cream of tartar), and also a drying agent (usually starch). Baking powder is available as single-acting baking powder and as double-acting baking powder. Double-acting powders react in two phases and can stand for a while before baking. With double-acting powder, some gas is released at

room temperature when the powder is added to the batter or dough, but the majority of the gas is released in the heat of the oven. You probably have double-acting baking powder in your pantry.

11. **Using coconut:** Packaged coconut (sweetened or unsweetened, shredded or flaked, dry or moist) can be found with baking ingredients in the store and need to be refrigerated once opened. If you do not use in 2 to 3 months, the next time you need coconut you will need to purchase a fresh bag. If you need toasted coconut for a recipe, spread in a single layer on a parchment-lined rimmed baking sheet and bake in a low, 325-degree oven for 5 to 7 minutes (watch closely as it burns quickly).

12. **Does spacing matter on your cookie sheet?** The quick answer is *yes*! Recipes will tell you how to space and it is important to pay attention to the suggestions. For example, if cookies have a lot of butter they will tend to spread out more. I once made a sheet of cookies and spaced them too close and when I took out the cookie sheet, I had one BIG cookie—not exactly what I was hoping for! In addition, pay attention to size of cookie dough you are placing on the sheet for the same reason. With some recipes, you may be able to put 15 to 20 cookies on one sheet without any problems. My suggestion is to make a test batch and see what happens and how your dough reacts.

13. **Spices! Spices! Spices!** Spices, both whole and ground, have a shelf life, although it is longer than some people might imagine. Spices do not go bad in the sense of becoming rancid or spoiled, but they do lose potency and complex layers of flavor. When spices lose their power, they should be discarded and replaced with fresh ones. Whole spices will keep the longest, because they have not been cracked or ground. They can last up to four years in an airtight container in a cool, dry place, and keep even better in the dark. Extremely strong spices such as whole cloves, cinnamon, and nutmeg may last even longer. How can you tell that whole spices are too old to use? When they have lost their aroma.

    Ground spices have a shorter shelf life, usually between two and three years. They should also be stored in a cool, dry place in airtight containers. To determine whether or not ground spices are still usable, gently shake the container with the cap on. Remove the cap after a moment and sniff to see if the rich smell of the spice is still present.

14. **Know your oven:** Oven temperatures vary and it is important to know how accurate your oven is. You can purchase an inexpensive oven thermometer and test out your oven. If your oven runs hot, simply adjust the temperature. I test my oven about once a year just to see if anything has changed. Turn your oven on at 350 degrees and leave on for 30 minutes or so and then check the thermometer; it will tell the tale.

15. How big is a pinch, dollop, splash, scant?

Pinch. The amount of dry spice or salt you can hold between your thumb and forefinger—no mystery here. The size of the pinch can purposely vary; a large pinch of salt in cookie dough keeps the cookies from tasting ho-hum flat; a small pinch of ground chipotle pepper in a salad dressing adds a slightly smoky edge without cranking up the heat too high.

Dollop. A little blob of a soft food, such as a mounded spoon of whipped cream plopped on a piece of pie, as an edible garnish.

Knob. A rounded nugget of a harder food, such as "a 2-inch knob of fresh ginger," to be sliced or grated.

Scant. Slightly less than the full amount. For a scant teaspoon, fill the measuring teaspoon with spice or salt, level the top, and then shake a bit off before adding to a dish.

Splash. A dash of a liquid; some chefs place a thumb over half of a bottle's opening and give the bottle a quick inverted turn, so only a few teaspoons are spread over a surface, such as a splash of Grand Marnier showered over strawberry halves. You might use more liquid if deglazing a pan because most of it will evaporate with heat.

16. Condensed milk: Condensed milk, also known as sweetened condensed milk, is cow's milk from which

water has been removed and to which sugar has been added, yielding a very thick, sweet product that can last for years without refrigeration if unopened. The two terms, condensed milk and sweetened condensed milk have become synonymous. Condensed milk is used in numerous dessert dishes in many countries. Do not confuse with **evaporated milk,** also known as dehydrated milk, which is a shelf-stable canned milk product with about 60 percent of the water removed from fresh milk, and with no added sugar.

17. **Brown sugar, light or dark.** Brown sugar gets it color from the addition of molasses. There are two varieties: Light brown sugar has 3.5 percent molasses and dark brown sugar has 6.5 percent molasses.

    Most recipes call for light brown sugar, but if you prefer the richer flavor of the dark, it can be used without a problem. When a recipe calls for firmly packed brown sugar, heap the sugar into a measuring cup and press down firmly to make level.

    Natural brown sugar is a name for **raw sugar,** which is a brown sugar produced from the first crystallization of the sugar cane. Natural brown sugar is free of additional dyes and chemicals. There is more molasses in natural brown sugar, giving it a higher mineral content. Some natural brown sugars have particular names and characteristics, and are sold as turbinado, muscovado, or Demerara sugar.

    Brown sugar must be stored in an airtight container or it can become too hard to work with. If you open your container and you discover that your brown sugar has become hard as a rock, do not despair. You have a couple of options. You can put in a piece of fresh bread or a slice of fresh apple. In a day or two, your brown sugar will be back to its perfect consistency. Another option is to purchase a clay medallion, sold in kitchen supply stores, that you soak in water for 15 to 20 minutes and put in your brown sugar container to prevent it from becoming too hard to work with.

18. **Sanding sugar:** Sanding sugar is a large-crystal sugar used as an edible decoration that will not dissolve when subjected to heat. Also called pearl sugar or decorating sugar, sanding sugar adds sparkle to cookies, baked goods, and candies. The sparkling effect is achieved because the grains of sugar are large and reflect light.

19. **Cocoa:** There are two kinds of cocoa powder that you will see used in recipes. Both types are unsweetened and bitter when tasted on their own (even though they smell sooooo good!)

    Dutch-process cocoa has been treated with an alkali to neutralize its acidity and therefore does not react with baking soda. It generally must be used in recipes calling for baking powder. It has a reddish brown color, mild flavor, and dissolves easily in liquids.

    Unsweetened cocoa has a more complex chocolate flavor than Dutch-process. Its more intense flavor makes it perfect for brownies, cookies, and chocolate cakes. When natural cocoa, which is acidic, is used in recipes with baking soda, it creates a leavening action that makes the batter rise in the oven.

20. **How to melt chocolate:** There are a few fundamental guidelines to successfully melting chocolate:

   * Make sure the chocolate is chopped into uniform pieces. Never try to melt large bars or blocks of chocolate that have not been chopped.

   * Avoid all contact with water! Make sure your bowls, workstation, and spatulas are completely dry.

   * Melt the chocolate slowly over low heat. Chocolate is very delicate and can become lumpy or grainy if overheated.

   * Stir the chocolate frequently with a rubber spatula.

   * Chocolate retains its shape when melted, so the only way to know if it is truly melted is to stir it. Do not rely on appearances alone.

MELTING CHOCOLATE IN THE MICROWAVE

THE MICROWAVE IS A GREAT tool for melting chocolate. It melts chocolate more quickly than a double boiler with minimal effort and mess. The most critical part of melting chocolate in the microwave is choosing an appropriate container. Ideally, you want to melt your chocolate in a microwave-safe bowl that remains cool after several minutes of near-continuous microwaving. It is preferable to melt your chocolate on a low (50%) power setting, to avoid burning it. If your microwave does not have this option, heat the chocolate in shorter intervals and stir each time. Additionally, if your microwave does not have a turntable, manually turn the bowl each time you stop and stir the chocolate.

It is very difficult to determine exact microwaving times, as it can vary depending on microwave wattage, quantity of chocolate, and even the cocoa butter content of the chocolate. However, as a rough guide, estimate about 1 minute for 1 ounce of chocolate, 3 minutes for 8 ounces of chocolate, 3.5 minutes for 1 pound of chocolate, and 4 minutes for 2 pounds. Run the microwave in 30-second to 1-minute increments, stirring in between and rotating the bowl if necessary. Finish heating when most, but not all, of the chocolate is melted. Stir the chocolate continuously until it is smooth, shiny, and completely melted.

MELTING CHOCOLATE IN A DOUBLE BOILER

THE TRADITIONAL METHOD OF MELTING chocolate is to use a double boiler. A double boiler is a specialized set of pans consisting of a saucepan that holds hot water, and a bowl that fits securely over the saucepan. Chocolate is placed in the top bowl and allowed to melt over gentle, indirect heat. If you don't own a double boiler, any metal or glass bowl that fits snugly over the top of a saucepan can be used.

You want enough water to provide heat, but not so much that the bottom of the chocolate bowl touches the water. Heat the saucepan over low heat until it just begins to simmer, then turn off the stove and place the chocolate bowl over the water. Let the chocolate begin to melt, and then stir it gently with a spatula. When almost all of the chocolate is melted, lift the top bowl from the saucepan and set it on the counter. Stir continuously until it is shiny, smooth, and completely melted.

21. **Candy Thermometer:** A candy thermometer is a thermometer used to measure the temperature and therefore the stage of a cooking sugar solution. It is a *must* for making candy. These thermometers can also be used to measure hot oil for deep-frying.

    There are several kinds of candy thermometers available. These include traditional liquid thermometers, coil spring dial thermometers, and digital thermometers. The digital thermometers tend to read the temperature more quickly and accurately, and some models have an alarm when the thermometer hits a certain temperature. Many models have markers for the various stages of sugar cooking.

    Cook the candy as directed. Some recipes will give you a temperature to aim for, while others may use one of the following terms: Thread, Soft Ball,

Medium Ball, Firm Ball, Hard Ball, Very Hard Ball, Soft Crack, Hard Crack, or Caramelized Sugar stages. The temperatures for some or most of these terms should be indicated on your candy thermometer. Place the candy thermometer in the pan with the cooking candy. Be sure the bulb of the thermometer never touches the bottom of the pan, or the temperature will register too high. You want to find out the temperature of the candy mixture, not of the pan.

Thread (begins at 230 degrees) Makes a long thread when dropped in cold water.

Soft Ball (234 degrees) Forms a soft ball that doesn't hold its shape. Cream candies, fudge, and fondants are done at the Soft Ball stage.

Firm Ball (246 degrees) This ball will only flatten with pressure. Divinity and caramels.

Hard Ball (250 degrees) This ball will hold its shape when pressed. Taffy.

Soft Crack (270–290 degrees) Separates into bendable threads. Toffee and butterscotch.

Hard Crack (300 degrees) Peanut brittle.

Caramelized Sugar (310 degrees)

APPENDIX I

Steps in Making Cookies

1. Preheat your oven to proper temperature.

2. Arrange all needed equipment conveniently.

3. Assemble all ingredients.

4. If chocolate is to be used, put to melt over hot water.

5. Prepare the cookie sheets or pans.

6. Sift flour once and measure (if using sifted flour).

7. Measure other dry ingredients.

8. Prepare fruits and nuts if being used, and measure.

9. Measure butter and other wet ingredients.

10. Cream the butter in the mixing bowl. *Never* melt the butter as this injures the texture. Butter is best used at room temperature.

11. Add sugar gradually and beat well with each addition.

12. Flavoring extracts are better distributed if added to liquid ingredients.

13. Eggs are usually well beaten before being added to creamed mixture. For a small amount of egg, just add directly to creamed mixture. If a lot of eggs, add to liquids then add alternately with the dry ingredients.

14. Nuts and fruits should be added last.

Handy Kitchen Math and Chemistry

EQUIVALENT MEASURES

1 tablespoon	=	3 teaspoons
2 tablespoons	=	1 fluid ounce
4 tablespoons	=	¼ cup or 2 ounces
5⅓ tablespoons	=	⅓ cup
8 tablespoons	=	½ cup (1 stick butter = 8 tablespoons)
1 cup	=	½ pint or 8 fluid ounces
2 cups	=	1 pint or 16 fluid ounces
4 cups	=	1 quart
4 quarts	=	1 gallon

ABBREVIATIONS

t	=	teaspoon
tsp	=	teaspoon
T	=	tablespoon
Tbsp	=	tablespoon
C	=	cup
oz	=	ounce
pkg	=	package
pt	=	pint
qt	=	quart
gal	=	gallon
lb	=	pound
#	=	pound

EMERGENCY DAIRY SUBSTITUTIONS

Buttermilk, 1 cup — 1 tablespoon vinegar or lemon juice plus enough milk to make 1 cup. Let mixture stand for 5 minutes.

Sour cream, 1 cup — 1 cup plain yogurt

Half-and-half, 1 cup — ⅞ cup milk plus 3 tablespoons butter

Yogurt (plain), 1 cup — 1 cup sour cream or buttermilk

Eggs, 2 large — 3 small eggs

Whole milk, 1 cup — ½ cup evaporated milk plus ½ cup water

Asiago — Parmesan cheese

Ricotta — Cottage cheese

Light cream, 1 cup — ⅞ cup milk plus 2 tablespoons butter

Cottage cheese, 1 cup, puréed — 1 cup sour cream

Mayonnaise, 1 cup (for salad dressings) — ½ cup plain yogurt and ½ cup mayonnaise or 1 cup sour cream or 1 cup puréed cottage cheese

EMERGENCY BAKING PRODUCT SUBSTITUTIONS

Active dry yeast, 1 package

2½ teaspoons dry or ⅓ cake yeast, crumbled

Baking powder, 1 teaspoon

¼ teaspoon baking soda plus ½ teaspoon cream of tartar

Cake flour, 1 cup

1 cup minus 2 tablespoons all-purpose flour, sifted

Cornstarch, 1 tablespoon (for thickening)

2 tablespoons flour (simmer about 3 minutes *after* the mixture has thickened)

Flour, 1 tablespoon (for thickening)

1½ teaspoons cornstarch

Honey, 1 cup

1¼ cup sugar plus ¼ cup liquids

Tapioca, 1 tablespoon (for thickening)

1½ tablespoons all-purpose flour

Cream of tartar, 1 teaspoon

1 tablespoon lemon juice or vinegar

Confectioners' sugar, 1 cup

1 cup sugar plus 1 tablespoon cornstarch, processed

Baking soda	There is *no* substitute for baking soda
Butter	Margarine or vegetable shortening (for baking only)
Shortening, 1 cup	1 cup softened butter or 1 cup margarine minus ½ teaspoon salt from recipe

SOURCES

Information on the history of cookies is from:

Davidson, Alan, *The Oxford Companion to Food* (New York: Oxford University Press, 1999).

Smith, Andrew F., *The Oxford Encyclopedia of Food and Drink in America* (New York: Oxford University Press, 2004).

Watts, Nellie, *The Cookie Book* (Pennsylvania: Culinary Arts Press, 1939).

Acknowledgments

FIRST AND FOREMOST, WE WANT to acknowledge each other because writing this book has been a collaborative joy. Though we've been close friends for well over a decade, we've come to appreciate each other's talent, strength, and humor at an entirely new level. This book has taught us magnificent things about each other.

Of course, we need to thank the bitches in our cookie club, not only for their excitement and support, but also for the great recipes and appetizers included in this book. We still have many "original" cookie bitches who are founding members: Karin Blazier, Daphne Mead Derbyshire, Kendra Hires, Linda Sotirion, Mary Jane (MJ) McKee, and Pamela Grates. We've seen a few changes over the years, adding Corey Crittenden, Sally Wisotzkey, Wendy Raymond, and our newest "virgin," Joan Curran, to the group. We're a super committed bunch who love our cookie club and I expect we'll still be making cookies twenty years from now! Many other friends gave us recipes and diligently (and willingly!) taste-tested numerous cookie recipes. Their suggestions follow in these pages. We're lucky to be surrounded by such fabulous and supportive bakers.

Two important things happened that made this book possible.

Gini Elliott stepped up to the plate and rescued us with her fabulous word processing. She had to learn to read handwritten pages, which she did brilliantly! Second is the inclusion of the well-kept-secret recipe for Peanut Brittle by Mary Helen Tolles, Marybeth's mother. We received the blessing from all her children so we could include this beloved recipe: Sandy Wilson, Carole Root, Pati Tolles, Gini Elliott, and Tom Tolles. They agreed this delicious peanut brittle must live on in these pages to be enjoyed by many generations to come. The recipe is just too wonderful not to share. It is one of the ways that Marybeth's mother lives on in our hearts.

Ruth Behar, as always, made many helpful suggestions along the way. The staff at the William L. Clements Library provided enthusiasm and pointed us to helpful books and articles. *The Oxford Companion to Food* by Alan Davidson, *The Oxford Encyclopedia of Food and Drink in America* edited by Andrew F. Smith, and *The Cookie Book* by Nellie Watts all contributed to the great flavors you'll find. Emily Bestler, Laura Stern, and Alysha Bullock helped form and finally bake the dough of our words into this book. Thank you for making it so easy for us. And a special thanks to Peter Miller, our literary manager, for helping to cook up this wonderful idea.

Index

bake-off, of molasses cookies,
66, 67–68
baking sheets, *see* cookie sheets
baking soda and baking
powder, 193–94
cocoa powder and, 198,
199
emergency substitutions for,
208, 209
baking tips, 189–202
baking one sheet at a time,
38
baking soda and baking
powder, 193–94
blanching almonds, 71
brown sugar, 197–98
candy thermometers and
stages in cooking sugar
solution, 201–2
checking oven temperature,
195
cocoa, 198–99
coconut, 194
condensed milk, 196–97
cooling cookie sheets
between batches, 38
dusting with confectioners'
sugar, 190
gathering ingredients, 38
lining baking sheets with
parchment paper,
190–91
margarine vs. butter,
191–92
measurement terminology
(pinch, dollop, know,
scant, and splash), 196

melting chocolate, 82–83,
199–201
oats and oatmeal, 193
preheating oven, 38
sanding sugar, 198
shortbread, 191
sifting flour, 189
spacing cookie dough on
cookie sheets, 194
spices, 195
steps in making cookies,
203–4
toasting coconut, 194
toasting nuts, 190
vanilla and other flavoring
extracts, 192
zesting citrus fruits,
189–90
Balls, Peanut Butter, 82–83
banana chips, in Crispy
Chocolate Jumbles,
58–59
bar cookies, 37, 121–28
Brown Butter Hazelnut
Shortbread with Fleur
de Sel, 124–26
cookie exchange's rule
about, 21–22, 37
Hazelnut Shortbread Sticks,
127–28
Seven-Layer Bars, 123
blue cheese, in Bacon-
Wrapped Dates
(*Datiles con Beicon*),
162
*Boston Cooking-School
Cook Book*, 33

Crinkles, Peanut Butter, 70
Crispy Chocolate Jumbles,
    58–59
cutouts, *see* rolled cookies

fruits:

    adding to other ingredients, 204

    citrus, zesting, 189–90

    preparing, 203

    see also specific fruits

Fudge, Mom's Friday Night, 139

G

George's Love Cookies, 55–56

gingerbread, 32–33

Ginger Carrot Soup, Roasted, 171–72

gingersnaps, 33

Glaze, 103–4

Goat Cheese, Pear Salad with Walnuts and, 164

gooey cookies, rule about, 21–22

graham cracker crumbs, in Seven-Layer Bars, 123

Green Chili Quiche, 168

Guacamole, Mild, 161

guests:

    choosing, 12–13, 14–15

    commitment expected of, 22–23

    life membership of, 23–24

    limiting number of, 13, 22

    sending invitations to, 17–18

    sending reminder e-mails to, 18, 20

H

half-and-half, emergency substitution for, 207

hand-formed cookies, *see* molded or hand-formed cookies

"hard ball," use of term, 202

"hard crack," use of term, 202

hazelnut(s):

    Brown Butter Shortbread with Fleur de Sel, 124–26

    Raspberry Linzer Cookies, 107–8

    Shortbread Sticks, 75–76, 127–28

    skinning, 76

hermit cookies, 34

Hershey, Milton, 33

Hershey Kisses, in Peanut Butter Crinkles, 70

history of cookies, 31–34

honey, 31, 32

    emergency substitution for, 208

hospice, donating cookies to, 26

hostesses of cookie exchanges:

    blessings and trials for, 18–20

    newbie, advice for, 19–20

    pre-party set-up and, 157–58

Hungarian Mushroom Soup, 175–76

N

Q

R

raisins:
  as decoration, 156
  Jubilee Jumbles, 53–54
  Raspberry Linzer Cookies,
    107–8
raw sugar, 197
Reese's peanut butter chips,
    in Chocolate-Covered
    Peanuts, 136
refrigerator cookies (icebox
    or slice-and-bake
    cookies), 34, 36,
    85–99
  Basic Refrigerator Cookies,
    87–88
  Chocolate-Nut Wafers,
    93–94
  Cranberry-Cherry
    Pinwheels, 95–97
  freezing, 151
  Nut-Edged Lemon Slices,
    98–99
  Orange Pistachio Slices,
    89–90
  Ultimate Double
    Chocolate Cookies,
    91–92
re-gifting:
  cookies from exchange,
    24–25
  packages, 149
reminder e-mails, 18, 20
Rice Krispies, in Crispy
    Chocolate Jumbles,
    58–59

ricotta, emergency substitution
    for, 207
Roasted Carrot Ginger Soup,
    171–72
rolled cookies (cutouts), 36,
    101–10
  Chocolate-Dipped Espresso
    Shortbread, 109–10
  decorating, 154
  Raspberry Linzer Cookies,
    107–8
  Santa Faces, 103–4
  Sugar Cookies, 105–6
Royal Icing, 105–6, 154
rubber spatulas, 40
rules for cookie exchanges,
    20–27
  bar cookies, 21–22, 37
  charity, 25–27
  commitment, 22–23
  cookie variety, 20–21
  enhancing fun, 27
  exclusive membership, 22
  life membership, 23–24
  no goo, 21–22
  packaging, 24–25
sharing a dish, 25

S

St. Louis World's Fair (1904),
    33
salads:
  Mandarin Orange, 177
  Pear, with Walnuts and
    Goat Cheese, 164